A WINDOW ON TOMORROW

A WINDOW ON TOMORROW

LIAM GOLIGHER

CHRISTIAN FOCUS PUBLICATIONS

© 1994 Liam Goligher
ISBN 1-85792-080-5

Published by
Christian Focus Publications Ltd
Geanies House, Fearn, Ross-shire,
IV20 1TW, Scotland, Great Britain.

Cover design by Donna Macleod

Scripture quotations are from the New International Version, published by Hodder and Stoughton.

Printed and bound in Great Britain by
Cox & Wyman Ltd, Reading, Berkshire

Contents

Introduction

The world scene has witnessed dramatic changes over the past few years. The collapse of communism and the rise of nationalism, economic instability and a global ecological crisis, have left many people feeling insecure and anxious about the future.

The burgeoning New Age movement has popularised astrology and channelling as means of looking ahead into tomorrow. The language of reincarnation and karma has crept into ordinary daily conversation for many people in the west.

In this situation, the church has been strangely silent. Afraid of the criticism about being so 'heavenly minded we are of no earthly use' we have opted not to speak about heaven at all. The pressure to appear relevant has forced us to package and repackage the parts of our message which apply to the 'here and now' and to ignore or skim over what the Bible has to say about the 'there and then'.

Yet Christianity is a religion of hope. Christians are people who have been 'saved in hope' (Romans 8:24). Paul can argue that, 'If only in this life we have hope in Christ, we are to be pitied more than all men' (1 Corinthians 15:19) - in other words, 'if this is all there is to being a Christian then we are wasting our time.' The benefits and blessings of the Christian gospel which we receive now are only the 'shadow' of a greater reality, the down payment of an inheritance that is yet to be ours, the foretaste of good things to come. Christians are people who live between the times, between Christ going and Christ coming. The universal faith of the church is this: 'Christ has died, Christ is risen, Christ will come again.'

It is my conviction that both the world and the church need to hear what the Bible has to say about the next stage in the career of Jesus Christ. People who are struggling with the problem of evil in society and in themselves need to hear that there will be a time when evil and injustice will be resolved. Those who are struggling with sickness and are fearful of death need to know that these will not have the last word. And people who fear the gradual incineration of our planet through environmental irresponsibility need to be told that there is a future for our planet itself in the purposes of God.

The Bible's teaching about Jesus Christ's return is not given to make us escapists, but to help us endure the ups and downs, the advances and set-backs of life, secure in the conviction that God will have the final word. Jesus will reign until all his enemies are put under his feet and 'the earth will be filled with the knowledge of the Lord as the water covers the sea.'

1

ITS HISTORY

Amillennialism
Postmillennialism
Historic Premillennialism
Dispensationalism
The identity of Antichrist
The role of Israel
The Nature and Sequence of the Resurrection
Conclusion

1

There can be no doubt that from the very beginning Christians have universally held the conviction that Jesus Christ would return personally and visibly to end history, to judge the world and bring full salvation to his people. But that is where the unity stops. Over the years, several divergent interpretations have developed. These different interpretations don't question the fact of his return, but the details surrounding his coming again.

The point of divergence for each of these is a passage in Revelation 20 verses 1-7. There, John sees in his vision Satan taken hold of and bound for a 1000 years. Then certain individuals ('those who were beheaded for their testimony to Jesus') are said to live and reign with Christ for the 1000 years period. At the end of this time (called the millennium from the Latin for thousand, mille) Satan is loosed, he deceives the nations and leads a demonic-human army against 'the camp of the saints and the beloved city' (Jerusalem). He is then decisively routed, finally defeated and cast into the lake of fire. There is then a second resurrection and the final judgment.

In the centuries immediately following the apostolic age, the interpretation given to this came to be known as Premillennialism. Eusebius, for example, records that Papias, who had known some of the apostles, had taught that after the resurrection, the kingdom of Christ would be established on earth for a thousand years. Justin Martyr, in his dialogue with Trypho, wrote that Christians knew there would be a bodily resurrection and that they would live in and rule from Jerusalem for a thousand years. Irenaeus believed that Christ would reign on earth for a thousand years after his return, and said that he knew of certain elders who had heard the Apostle John say that this was what the Lord himself had taught. Many took up these views; some wondered whether the thousand years should be taken literally; while others put together wild and extravagant descriptions of the worldly joys of this period. These extreme views naturally provoked a reaction on the part of other orthodox teachers of the church.

Probably the most influential Christian in the period after the Apostolic age was St. Augustine of Hippo. He tells us that at first he was inclined to accept the literal view of a thousand year reign. His views changed however as he came to believe that the passage referred to the church age. The binding of Satan fulfilled the words in Mark 3:27, the thousand years was the period between Christ's first and second coming. The judgment given to the saints was the power of binding and loosing of sins which Jesus gave the church and the first resurrection was the spiritual rebirth in baptism. Augustine's view (known as Amillennialism – the negative 'a' indicating that its advocates reject the literal and earthly interpretation of the millennium) came to be the view held by the majority of the Reformers.

The Puritan period was a time of spiritual renewal in Great Britain and its colonies and led to a shift of emphasis in prophetic interpretation. There is no doubt that the 'success' of the gospel in that age stirred up optimism, but there was also greater attention given to passages like Romans 11 which speak of the ingathering of Jews and Gentiles into the church. The Puritans believed firmly that one should not underestimate the power of the gospel or the potential of Christ's present rule ultimately to transform dramatically men's social, political and international relations.

Thomas Goodwin (1600-1680) in one sermon says, 'There will come a time when the generality of mankind, both Jew and Gentile shall come to Jesus Christ. He hath had but little takings of the world yet, but he will have before he hath done.'

John Owen wrote: 'Though our persons fall, our cause shall be as truly, certainly and infallibly victorious, as that Christ sits at the right hand of God. The gospel shall be victorious. This greatly comforts and refreshes me.'

There is no doubt that it was such convictions that gave birth to the modern missionary movements. It undergirded William Carey's great summary of the prophet Isaiah's message: 'Expect great things from God. Attempt great things for God.' What kept Carey going was his assurance: 'He must reign, till Satan has not an inch of territory.' The view that 'the gospel will yet triumph' sent Carey to India; David Brainerd to the North American Indians; Robert Morrison to China; and David Livingstone to Africa. It inspired Isaac Watts to write such well established hymns as *Jesus shall reign where'er the sun*.

The nineteenth century saw the rise of yet another prophetic perspective. The influence of rationalism had emptied much of formal Christianity of its belief in the supernatural and as a result, had eroded the hopes of many in the personal return of Christ. The belief in the triumph of the gospel bequeathed by the Puritans and their successors was perverted into a belief in mankind's inevitable progress. This humanistic view was supported by the emerging theory of evolution. Throughout the English-speaking world, there were groups of people who wanted to get back to basics. They took the Bible seriously and were attracted to the early church's belief in the personal and premillennial return of Christ. Many conferences and periodicals emerged which explored the themes of prophecy and Christ's imminent return. The most influential figure in this prophetic movement was an ex-Church of Ireland (Anglican) clergyman, J. N. Darby.

Darby formulated a new system of interpretation known as dispensationalism. Dispensationalism saw the promise of a literal kingdom of God to the Jews as the key issue in prophetic interpretation. The church age was a blip - a parenthesis - in God's real purpose to restore the kingdom to Israel with Messiah Jesus reigning over an idealised Jewish State in Jerusalem.

So the prophetic plan was this: the imminent and secret return of Jesus and the removal of his church to heaven (called the Rapture); the return of the Jews to Palestine; the Great Tribulation (connected to the seventieth week of Daniel 9:20-27) where the world goes out of control due to the absence of the Spirit's restraining activity; the emergence of Antichrist; the persecution of the Jews; the uniting of nations and their convergence on Israel with a view to destroying her; the return of Christ in public with his angels and his church to wage war on the nations at Armageddon and establish his throne in Jerusalem for a 1000 year period.

Darby took this view to North America where it took a firm root among evangelical believers. Dispensationalism was popularised through the notes in the famous Scofield Reference Bible. Defenders of this view have been among the most vociferous sponsors of the national restoration of Israel. They see this as a significant step forward in God's prophetic programme.

So much for the history, what do these various viewpoints teach?

Amillennialism

According to Amillennialism, the reign of Christ began upon his ascension and with the outpouring of the Holy Spirit at Pentecost. Since that time, he has continued to exercise his royal power through the influence of the gospel and the work of his Spirit upon the minds and hearts of men. The thousand years in Revelation 20 is to be understood as a symbolic way of describing a very long rule of Christ. In support of this, they cite the symbolic use of numbers throughout Revelation and the lack of any direct reference anywhere else in Scripture to a thousand year reign. Right now, they say, Satan is bound in that his work is hindered by the power of the gospel and the spiritual lordship of Christ. The first resurrection is interpreted as the new birth (or as the resurrection of Christ in which the believer has a part through the new birth).

The Amillennialist also claims that many of the Old Testament prophecies relating to Israel have either been fulfilled historically (many of them before the birth of Christ), or spiritually in the New Testament church. For example, the promise of the land of Canaan made to Abraham was fulfilled in the conquest under Joshua and in the reign of David. And the prophecies of a return to the land and a renewal of God's blessings upon the nation of Israel were fulfilled literally, according to the Amillennialist, in the return of many Jews to their land in 538 BC following the Babylonian exile. They would also argue that many of the titles and privileges given to Israel in the old covenant are ascribed to the church under the new. The church is 'the holy nation' (1 Peter 2:9) and 'the Israel of God' (Galatians 6:16); therefore, there are no more plans or purposes for Israel as a nation distinct from any other nation.

In summary, Amillennialists believe that the rule of Christ is a present spiritual reality in the hearts and minds of God's people. They do not expect a future political manifestation of it in a millennial kingdom. They look for a progression in evil toward the close of this present age. As men turn away from God and become unreceptive to the gospel, the world is prepared for the appearance of the Man of Sin, or Antichrist. They understand the Second Coming as a single event followed by a general resurrection of both believers and unbelievers. After gathering together his people at the 'rapture', Christ will judge the world from the Great White Throne, and then usher in the blessings of the new heaven and new earth.

Postmillennialism

Perhaps the best description of post-millennialism has been given by Lorraine Boettner:

> 'Postmillennialism is that view of the last things which holds that the Kingdom of God is now being extended in the world through the preaching of the gospel and the saving work of the Holy Spirit in the hearts of individuals, that the world eventually is to be Christianised and that the return of Christ is to occur at the close of a long period of righteousness and peace commonly called the millennium.'

According to this view, the present age will gradually merge into the millennial age as an increasingly larger proportion of the world's inhabitants are converted to Christianity through the preaching of the gospel. This growing number of Christians will include both Jews and Gentiles. Postmillennialists generally understand Romans 11:25-26 as teaching a future large-scale conversion of the Jewish people, though they don't think of this as involving a restoration of a Jewish political kingdom.

During the millennium, Christian values and standards will be accepted by nations and individuals. Not that everyone will become a Christian or that sin will be eliminated, but that the social, moral, cultural, economic and political life of mankind will be vastly improved. The earth's resources will be shared out more equitably and there will be justice for all.

Historic Premillennialism

The Premillennialist along with the Amillennialist insists that the world is evil, that the business of the church primarily is to preach the gospel of salvation and that the Christian must be living in constant expectation of the personal second coming of Christ. The fullness of the kingdom will come only with the coming of the King.

Historic Premillennialists believe that a number of events must happen before Christ comes back: the evangelisation of the nations, the Great Tribulation, the great apostasy or rebellion and the appearance of a personal Antichrist. When Christ does return, it will be suddenly and decisively, in public and with great splendour; he will restore his people and show them off before a watching world in their resurrected and transformed humanity.

Christ and the saints will then descend to the earth. Antichrist's oppressive reign will be ended. Either at this time or just before, the vast majority of Jews will repent and put their trust in Jesus as Messiah to the blessing of the world.

The millennial kingdom will then be established with Christ and his people ruling visibly over the entire world. Evil will be greatly restrained, unbelieving nations will be kept in check and ruled over by Christ with a rod of iron. It will be a time of social, political and economic justice and of great peace and prosperity. Earth will be unusually productive and the desert will blossom as the rose. Support for this view, apart from Revelation 20, is drawn from passages which describe the kingdom as an ideal earthly order (Psalm 50:2-5; Micah 4:1-3; Isaiah 11:1-10; 35:1-10; 65:17-25; Zechariah 14:9, 16-17).

Dispensationalism

Dispensationalism, as we noted earlier, arose in the writings of J. N. Darby (1800-1882) in the 19th century. It shares with historic Premillennialism a belief that Christ will reign on earth for a thousand years after his return.

Dispensationalism teaches an absolute distinction between Israel and the Church as two separate peoples of God. John Walvoord has written:

The Dispensationalist believes that throughout the ages God is pursuing two distinct purposes: one related to the earth with earthly people and earthly objectives involved, which is Judaism; while the other is related to heaven with heavenly people and heavenly objectives involved, which is Christianity... (*The Millennial Kingdom* pp vii-viii).

The New Scofield Reference Bible distinguishes seven successive historical periods or dispensations:

1. Innocence (Genesis 1-3: in the Garden);
2. Conscience (Genesis 3-7: Fall to the Flood);
3. Human Government (Genesis 8-11: the Flood to Abraham);
4. Promise (Abraham to Moses);
5. the Law (Moses to Christ);
6. the gospel (the first coming of Christ to his return);
7. the Kingdom (the millennial reign of Christ after his return).

A dispensation is defined as 'a period of time during which man is tested in respect to his obedience to some specific revelation of the will of God' (*New Scofield Reference Bible* p. 3 re. 3). Though in each dispensation God reveals his will in a different way, these dispensations are not separate ways of salvation. 'During each of them, man is reconciled to God in only one way, i.e. by God's grace through the work of Christ that was accomplished on the cross and vindicated in his resurrection' (ibid).

Jesus' first coming was with a view to offering the Jews the kingdom of God. When they rejected this offer, Christ then turned to the Gentiles and introduced the idea of the church. Some Dispensational teachers say that the present church age was not predicted in the Old Testament and is a 'parenthesis' in God's predicted program for Israel.

The second coming of Jesus will be in two stages separated by a seven year period. First he will come for his saints (the rapture), then he will come with his saints (the revelation). The rapture may occur at any moment: there are no prophecies to be fulfilled before it occurs and the first indication of it to the world will be the disappearance of Christians world-wide.

The rapture will be followed by a seven year period on earth (Daniel 9:24-27). During this period, the gospel of the kingdom will be preached throughout the world by those (principally Jews) who become believers due to the church's disappearance. There will be an unprecedented outburst of persecution against the people of God, 'the time of Jacob's trouble' (Jeremiah 30:7). Antichrist will emerge and will eventually gather a huge army together to attack the people of God in the Battle of Armageddon.

At this, Christ will return in glory, accompanied by his church, to destroy his enemies and to establish his throne in Jerusalem. The millennial reign of Christ will fulfil the national promises made to Israel in the Old Testament. The millennium will be a golden age such as the world has never seen before. The earth will be full of the knowledge of God as the waters cover the sea. Worship in the millennium will centre round a rebuilt temple in Jerusalem, to which all nations will go to offer praise to God. Animal sacrifices will be once again offered at the temple. These sacrifices, however, will not be propitiatory offerings (to deal with sin), but memorial offerings, in remembrance of Christ's death.

These are the different viewpoints held among evangelical Christians today. Apart from the issue of the millennium itself which is in dispute, there are several other matters that promote discussion.

The identity of Antichrist

The clearest teaching about Antichrist is to be found in John's letters. In 1 John 2:18, John says that we know it is the last hour because there are many antichrists. There is a spirit abroad in the world which denies the true God and the Christian claim that Jesus Christ is God manifest in the flesh.

We can expect this spirit of antichrist to continue to exert an underground influence through history until Christ returns.

There are indicators that towards the close of this age, false teachers, possessed and directed by evil spirits, will become more prominent (1 Timothy 4:1-3; 2 Timothy 3:1-9; 2 Peter 3:3-7; Jude 18,19). In addition to this, there is a strand of teaching which points to the emergence of a final expression of the spirit of Antichrist in a single figure at the time of the end. Daniel 7 records a vision of four great beasts and the rise of 'a little horn' (a political figure) which overthrows the others. This horn 'had eyes and a mouth that spoke great things and it made war with the saints, and prevailed over them, until the Ancient of Days came' (Daniel 7:20,21). Revelation 13 has various similarities to Daniel's vision of the beasts and the horns. Here though one of the beasts itself takes on the characteristics of Antichrist. It emerges out of the sea (verses 1-4), blasphemes God's name and is given universal authority (verses 5-10). It has a human number, 666, each digit falls short of the perfect number 7 and indicates human effort, human teaching and human nature which is repeated but fails to rise above itself.

2 Thessalonians 2 contains the clearest reference to a final and climactic embodiment of the spirit of Antichrist. Paul speaks of the coming of

'the man of lawlessness' who will 'oppose and will exalt himself over everything that is called God or is worshipped, so that he sets himself up in God's temple, proclaiming himself to be God' (2:3,4). Anthony Hoekema identifies a number of things that are said about 'the man of lawlessness' in this passage.

1) He will come out of the great apostasy or rebellion.

2) He will be a person.

3) He will be an object of worship. 'The temple of God' (verse 4) is variously interpreted as the Christian church, or a literal Jewish temple.

4) He will use deceptive miracles (verse 9) and false teaching (verse 11) to advance his cause.

5) He can only be revealed after that which restrains has been taken out of the way (verses 6,7). The 'restrainer' is said by some to be the Roman Empire or a series of emperors. Others, like John Calvin, have held that that which restrains is the preaching of the gospel to all nations. Dispensationalists commonly teach that the restrainer is the Holy Spirit.

6) The man of lawlessness will be totally overthrown by Christ at his second coming

(verse 8). (Anthony A. Hoekema *The Bible and the Future* Eerdmans pages 161, 162).

Christians over the centuries have identified Antichrist as Nero, Napoleon, Hitler, etc. In a sense they were right because such anti-God figures have expressed the spirit of antichrist in their age. But the fact that none of these was the final Antichrist figure shouldn't make us complacement. Rather the scriptures exhort us to be on the watch and to 'test the spirits' abroad in our own day, to see whether they are of God.

The role of Israel

The survival of the Jewish people for more than 3,500 years is one of history's great phenomena. Israel was originally chosen to be the channel of God's purposes in the world beginning with the call of Abraham in Genesis 12. Israel was called to be a light to the nations but manifestly failed in that mission. Yet from Israel emerged the Messiah to be the world's Saviour (Romans 9:4,5). As Jesus told the woman at the well, 'salvation is from the Jews' (John 4:22). But the Jews as a whole rejected their Messiah and refused the salvation that was freely offered them and the movement of God's salvation turned outwards to the Gentiles.

So the question is: Has God finished with Israel? Certainly there are many Bible teachers that think so. Alan Stibbs wrote: 'When Christ died, the order of things under the old Israel ceased to be and their inevitable dissolution followed. When Christ was raised from the dead a new Israel was begun in him'; and again, 'The New Testament nowhere promises an earthly, national future either for the Jewish race or for Palestine and Jerusalem. Its whole hope and sure promise of fulfilment are concentrated on the spiritual Israel and the heavenly Jerusalem. For the former were but the temporary figure; the latter are the eternally true' (Alan Stibbs *God's Church* IVP pp 53, 59).

Others, however, are convinced that Israel has a future role in God's purposes. Dispensationalists believe that after the rapture of the church, God will again turn his attention to Israel. The nation as a whole will be converted, whether just before Christ returns or at the very moment of his coming. Others look for a future conversion of Israel as a nation, or of the Jews as a people, with untold blessing for the world.

Certainly, Romans 11:24-32 points to a future act of mercy on God's part by which the entire nation will be restored to God. There Paul argues first that God's rejection of Israel is not complete - some Jews, like Paul himself, are being converted. Second, God's rejection of Israel isn't arbitrary - they have brought it on themselves by their unbelief and disobedience. Third, God's rejection of Israel isn't final. Here, Paul contrasts the 'remnant' that has been saved with the 'fullness' that will yet be saved.

The very existence of Israel as a nation (albeit still in unbelief) is a witness to God's preserving mercy. But if Romans 11 is taken seriously, Israel's future has to be a gospel future if it is to have eternal significance. We should hope and pray 'for a significant turning to the Lord Jesus Christ on the part of many Jewish people with resulting blessing for the world-wide church' (Bruce Milne, *The End of the World*, Kingsway p. 77).

The Nature and Sequence of the Resurrection
Christianity is unique in its expectation of a resurrection of the body. The resurrection of Jesus himself becomes, in the New Testament, the ground and guarantee of the believer's resurrection. The Greeks believed that the body is evil and that it is a hindrance to man's full existence. So at death, the body disintegrates while the soul lives on. The early Christians were swimming against the intellectual current with their talk of a resurrection of the dead.

Among Christians, much discussion has taken place about the question of the time of the resurrection. There is no dispute about its relation to the coming of Christ. Premillennialists remind us that the first coming of Christ was a composite event

(comprising his birth, life, ministry, death, resurrection) and argue that his second coming will be
similar - the return, accompanied by the resurrection of believers, followed by the 1,000 year reign,
then the resurrection of unbelievers and the final
judgment. Dispensationalists speak of the second
advent in terms of the rapture (and resurrection of
believers); the seven year period predicted by
Daniel; the return to the Mount of Olives; the
millennium; the resurrection and judgment of unbelievers. Inherent in both these views is a two
stage resurrection of believers at the beginning of
the millennium and of unbelievers at the end.

Others point to such Scriptures as Daniel 12:2
and John 5:28-29 to argue for a general resurrection of believers and unbelievers at the moment of
Christ's return, followed immediately by final
judgment.

It is perhaps only fair to add that both views
regard the return of Christ as a composite event
involving the resurrection and rapture of the saints,
the resurrection of unbelievers, the return of Christ
to this planet, the judgment (or judgments) and the
reign of Christ (either in the millennium or in the
new heavens and earth or both).

As to the nature of the resurrection, the New
Testament teaching is far clearer than that of the
Old Testament. In the New Testament the hope of
our resurrection is firmly based on the resurrection

of Christ and the believer's resurrection body is modelled upon his (Romans 8:11,29; Philippians 3:20, 21). In the resurrection, the bodies of believers will become like the body of Christ's glory, from which all the results of sin, including death, will have been removed. 1 Corinthians 15 contains the clearest and fullest treatment of the subject. Paul uses the analogy of the relationship between a seed and a plant and between sowing and reaping to illustrate the relationship between our present body and our resurrection. He presents a series of contrasts between the two - corruption and incorruption; dishonour and glory; weakness and power; the natural (i.e. part of this sin-cursed existence) and the spiritual (i.e. totally dominated and directed by the Holy Spirit).

There will therefore be both discontinuity and continuity between our present body and our resurrection body. Gone forever will be the limitations of our current human situation. Gone will be the proneness to sin and the susceptibility to sickness, disease and death. There will be unimaginable new powers and new possibilities. But at the same time, there will be continuity. It is 'we' who shall be changed. If there was no continuity, there would be no point in having a resurrection at all. The calling into existence of an entirely new set of people would not be a resurrection. No, the evidence points to our being both recognisable and different. The same people but marvellously changed. The experience of resurrection will be wonderful beyond our highest imaginings.

Conclusion

In this chapter, then, we have tried to set out some of the differences in detail among those who believe in the personal return of Jesus Christ. We mustn't allow these differences to cause a breach in our fellowship or to obscure the unanimous conviction among Bible believing folk in our Lord's return. Instead, I would suggest that each of these views has made a unique contribution to the church at large.

Amillennialism has taught us to take the church seriously. The church age is not a blip in God's plan, but an essential part of his purposes. Christian people are the children of Abraham by faith and the church has been grafted into the Israel of God. God's final purpose is to reconcile all things together in Christ and to re-create a new heaven and a new earth. Amillennialism focuses on our legacy from the past.

Postmillennialism urges us to take seriously the need to get the gospel out to the world and to believe that there are yet greater triumphs for the gospel to come before Christ returns. It challenges us to believe that the Christian message can still make significant inroads into the structures of this present world system. It faces us with the need to stake the claims of Christ on every aspect of human life and endeavour, and not to assume that there is any part of human activity that is unredeemable. Postmillennialism focuses on our duty in the present.

Premillennialism has kept the second coming of Christ on the agenda of Christian thought. It has reminded us of the 'then and there' when we had become preoccupied with the 'here and now'. It has raised our expectations of a gospel future for Jewish people and its emphasis on the immanent return of Christ has challenged us to present holiness of life. And by making much of the rapture of believers and their reign with Christ on earth, they have sharpened our vision of the glories that are to come. Premillennialism focuses on our destiny in the future.

I would want to thank God for the unique insight of each of these views and to encourage each reader to search the scriptures for themselves and be persuaded in their own mind. Maybe, as you read through this book, you would like to hazard a guess about where the author is coming from? I'll leave that to you!

2

ITS CERTAINTY

The Word of God the Father
The Work of God the Son
The Witness of God the Holy Spirit

2

A story is told of the famous English agnostic, Thomas Huxley, who was visiting Ireland for some speaking engagements. On one occasion he was leaving his Dublin hotel in a hurry to catch a taxi to the train station in order to get to engagements in the north of Ireland. He thought that the doorman at the hotel had told the taxi-driver where he was to go, so he rushed out of the hotel, jumped into the taxi, and shouted to the driver to hurry up and get there as fast as he could.

A few minutes later he looked out the window, to realise that the taxi-driver was driving at breakneck speed in the opposite direction from the railway station. So he asked the taxi-driver if he knew where he was going. The taxi-driver replied, 'No, but I'm going as fast as I can.'

Now there is a sense in which that is a parable of our modern situation at the end of the twentieth century. The human race does not know where it is going, but it is going there at breakneck speed.

It isn't that people are not interested in the future. The New Age movement has as one of its spin-offs encouraged an interest in astrology. On prime-time television every morning in one of the breakfast shows an astrologer reads charts for the day.

In May 1988, there was a great furore in the USA because of the news that the Reagans used astrology forecasts in some of the international decisions that the President was making on behalf of the United States.

Politicians would love to have a window on tomorrow. At a private dinner held in the White House at the end of June 1990, Mikhail Gorbachev confided in one of the guests, 'We need a road-map for the future.' The comment of some of the businessmen there was: 'Nice to say, but tough to draw up.'

Faced as the world is with political upheaval, economic instability, global warming, environmental pollution, nuclear weaponry, all proliferating across the world, the future is a matter of concern. What does tomorrow hold? The question we are going to look at is: What does the Bible have to say in this confusion?

What is the Christian message about the future? Do we simply say what John Wesley said about the Christian people of his day — 'Our people die well.' Thank God this is true. Yet is that all we have to say about the future? No!

The Christian hope and expectation for the future has always been, and remains, this: Jesus Christ is coming again personally, visibly, for the universe to see. That is the focal point towards which all of history is moving today. The Christian hope differs from all human longings with regard to the future, because of the indelible stamp of certainty that is placed upon it. It is this certainty which I will examine in this chapter.

Why is it that Christians when they talk about the second coming of Jesus talk not in terms of vague speculation, but in terms of strong assurance? I am convinced that this certainty arises from the knowledge Christians have that each member of the Trinity, the Father, the Son and the Holy Spirit, has an involvement in the second coming of Christ. In stating it this way, I hope to fully show the basis of our hope.

The Word of God the Father
First of all, we believe in the certainty of Jesus' return because of the *word* of God the Father. He has given us his promise. This word of God, this promise of God, has been expressed in prophecy throughout the Old Testament Scriptures. Let me give a short conducted tour through the Old Testament.

We will go right back to the beginning of human

history, at the very moment when man fell into sin. In Genesis 3:15, God promises Eve that one of her descendants would be responsible, ultimately, for the destruction of the serpent that had enticed them into sin: 'And I will put enmity between you [the serpent] and the woman, and between your offspring and hers; he will crush your head, and you will strike his heel.' Admittedly it is a vague promise: but elsewhere in the Bible the serpent is identified as the devil, a fallen angel who rebelled against God and whose determination it is to destroy the work of God (see Revelation 12:9).

As we progress through the Old Testament we discover after the flood, when only Noah and his family were preserved from drowning under God's judgment, that this person was going to be one of the descendants of Shem. Later on, God promised that it was going to be Abraham's family line which would produce this coming one who was going to be responsible for the destruction of the devil:

> The LORD had said to Abram, 'Leave your country, your people and your father's household and go to the land I will show you.
>   'I will make you into a great nation
>   and I will bless you;
>   I will make your name great,
>   and you will be a blessing.

> I will bless those who bless you,
>> and whoever curses you I will curse;
> and all peoples on earth
>> will be blessed through you.'
> (Genesis 12:1-3)

Then in Psalm 2, David describes the coming one as the Son of God enthroned in the heavens. God the Father has installed his King in Zion. He has said to him,

> 'You are my Son; ...
> Ask of me,
>> and I will make the nations your inheritance,
>> the ends of the earth your possession.
> You will rule them with an iron sceptre;
>> you will dash them to pieces like pottery.'
> (verses 7-9)

Our last stop is at the prophet Daniel, who says in a vision:

> 'I looked, and there before me was one like a son of man coming with the clouds of heaven ... He was given authority, glory and sovereign power; all peoples, nations and men of every language worshipped him. His dominion is an everlasting dominion that will not pass away, and his kingdom is one that will never be destroyed.' (Daniel 7:13-14)

The Old Testament goes on to inform us that this coming one is going to be a prophet like Moses (Deuteronomy 18:18). He is going to be a king like David, belonging to the royal tribe of Judah (Genesis 49:8-10), in fact from David's family, born in David's town (Micah 5:2). He is going to be a priest, but unlike Eli's sons he will be a faithful priest who will offer a sacrifice for sin that is going to be effective for ever (1 Samuel 2:35).

Yet mysteriously, as we go through the Old Testament, we discover that this heir of the inheritance, this ruler that is to come, is going to be God's suffering servant (Isaiah 52:13-14). Suddenly the picture of the future becomes a bit obscure. How can this coming ruler who is going to rule the nations with a rod of iron, also be the suffering servant who is mistreated and despised and rejected of men, a man of sorrows and acquainted with grief? But that is what is said!

Ultimately, this coming ruler is going to establish the throne of David for ever, and will be victorious, finally, over all his enemies. Isaiah 11 is a good summary of what the Old Testament predicts:

A shoot will come up from the stump of Jesse;
from his roots a Branch will bear fruit.
The Spirit of the LORD will rest on him —
    the Spirit of wisdom and of understanding,

the Spirit of counsel and of power,
the Spirit of knowledge and of the fear of the
LORD —
and he will delight in the fear of the LORD.
He will not judge by what he sees with his eyes,
or decide by what he hears with his ears;
but with righteousness he will judge the needy,
with justice he will give decisions for the poor
of the earth.
He will strike the earth with the rod of his mouth;
with the breath of his lips he will slay the
wicked.
Righteousness will be his belt
and faithfulness the sash round his waist.

The wolf will live with the lamb,
the leopard will lie down with the goat,
the calf and the lion and the yearling together,
and a little child will lead them.
The cow will feed with the bear,
their young will lie down together,
and the lion will eat straw like the ox.
The infant will play near the hole of the cobra,
and the young child put his hand into the
viper's nest.
They will neither harm nor destroy
on all my holy mountain,
for the earth will be full of the knowledge of the
LORD
as the waters cover the sea.

In that day the Root of Jesse will stand as a banner
for the peoples; the nations will rally to him, and his
place of rest will be glorious (verses 1-10).

In these verses, the coming King is described as a
root out of the stump of Jesse; that was the family,
the royal family, of David. He is going to belong
to the house and line of David. He will bring about
universal judgment (verse 4), universal peace
(verses 6-9), and universal knowledge of God
(verse 9).

God the Father revealed that a King would
come who would rule the world in righteousness,
and bring about a renovation of creation that will
have cosmic, universal significance.

But this word of God that has been expressed in
prophecy has been *confirmed in history*. That is
why it gives a note of certainty to our hope of the
second coming of Jesus. If we just had this list of
predictions we might stand back and say, 'Well,
there is no reason for us to believe that these
predictions will come true.' But the fact of the
matter is that a whole series of these predictions
have already been fulfilled, to the letter, in the first
coming of the Lord Jesus.

When you read the New Testament writers, one
of the points they make over and over again is that
their book, the New Testament, is a book showing
that God's word has been fulfilled. Jesus Christ, in

his person, fulfilled prophecies, the last of which
had been made five hundred years before his
arrival on the scene.

Jesus, the Messiah, the Saviour, is born a Jew,
of the tribe of Judah, of David's line, in Bethlehem,
by a virgin, and is called a Nazarene (derived from
the Hebrew word for 'branch' in Isaiah 11, *nazar*).

He entered Jerusalem on a donkey, and was
betrayed for thirty pieces of silver as Zechariah had
said (9:9; 11:12-13). He was despised and rejected
of men as Isaiah had said (53:3). He was pierced in
his hands and his feet as the Psalmist had said
(22:16). He was buried among the rich, and raised
again from the dead (Isaiah 53:9,11).

On the basis of God's word in prophecy being
fulfilled in history, we believe in the certainty of
the second coming of Jesus. Since all of what God
promised in respect to his first coming came true,
all that God has promised with respect to his
second coming is also going to come true.

The Work of God the Son
The second plank in this certainty is with respect
to the work of God the Son.

We have to face up to Jesus Christ being a fact
of history. Every one in the world has ultimately to
make up his mind about Jesus Christ. He is an
historical person. Over three-quarters of the world
are prepared to admit that Jesus Christ is one of the

greatest prophets that ever lived. Muslims confess that freely. Others say Jesus Christ is one of the most radical teachers in the history of man. Christians are prepared to go further and say that Jesus is not only a great prophet and a great teacher, but he is also a great saviour.

I want to identify two roles that Jesus fulfilled when he came into the world. He came to be a teacher and he came to be a saviour. And in both those areas Jesus made it quite clear that his second coming was part of his plan.

Jesus as a Teacher

Some admirers of Jesus refer to the Sermon on the Mount; but at the end of the Sermon on the Mount we come face to face with his teaching about the future.

Others like some of the teaching of Jesus about the Kingdom of God. Yet Jesus taught that the Kingdom of God had come, and that the Kingdom of God was coming. It has yet to come in its fullness, in its consummation. It is one Kingdom, he taught, in two stages. The first stage of the coming Kingdom of God is secret, and hidden in the hearts and minds of all who put their faith in him. The second stage of the coming of the Kingdom will be public, open, manifest, for all the world to see.

The Kingdom of God is God's rule: now in the

hearts and minds of those who believe; then, publicly, for all the world to share. Take his illustrations - the parables that he told - in which he talks about his return. I select two of them.

First, the parable of the master who goes away from home:

'Who then is the faithful and wise servant, whom the master has put in charge of the servants in his household to give them their food at the proper time? It will be good for that servant whose master finds him doing so when he returns. I tell you the truth, he will put him in charge of all his possessions. But suppose that servant is wicked and says to himself, "My master is staying away a long time," and he then begins to beat his fellow-servants and to eat and drink with drunkards. The master of that servant will come on a day when he does not expect him and at an hour he is not aware of. He will cut him to pieces and assign him a place with the hypocrites, where there will be weeping and gnashing of teeth.' (Matthew 24:45-51)

He leaves his house in the hands of his servants, and he tells them to take care of it until he comes back. The time of his return is unknown. The danger is that the servant will be found unprepared for him when he comes back. Jesus says in verse 50, 'The master of that servant will come on a day when he does not expect him and at an hour he is not aware of.' Jesus was saying to his disciples, Although I am going to leave you, I am going to return again. When I come back I am going to evaluate what you have been doing in my world.

This is the same emphasis as the parable of the talents that Jesus taught:

Again, it [the kingdom of heaven] will be like a man going on a journey, who called his servants and entrusted his property to them. To one he gave five talents of money, to another two talents, and to another one talent, each according to his ability. Then he went on his journey. The man who had received the five talents went at once and put his money to work and gained five more. So also, the one with the two talents gained two more. But the man who had received the one talent went off, dug a hole in the ground and hid his master's money.

After a long time the master of those servants returned and settled accounts with them. The man who had received the five talents brought the other five. 'Master,' he said, 'you entrusted me with five talents. See, I have gained five more.'

His master replied, 'Well done, good and faithful servant! You have been faithful with a few things; I will put you in charge of many things. Come and share your master's happiness!'

The man with the two talents also came. 'Master,' he said, 'you entrusted me with two talents; see, I have gained two more.'

His master replied, 'Well done, good and faithful

servant! You have been faithful with a few things; I will put you in charge of many things. Come and share your master's happiness!'

Then the man who had received the one talent came. 'Master,' he said, 'I knew that you are a hard man, harvesting where you have not sown and gathering where you have not scattered seed. So I was afraid and went out and hid your talent in the ground. See, here is what belongs to you.'

His master replied, 'You wicked, lazy servant! So you knew that I harvest where I have not sown and gather where I have not scattered seed? Well then, you should have put my money on deposit with the bankers, so that when I returned I would have received it back with interest.

'Take the talent from him and give it to the one who has the ten talents. For everyone who has will be given more, and he will have an abundance. Whoever does not have, even what he has will be taken from him. And throw that worthless servant outside, into the darkness, where there will be weeping and gnashing of teeth.' (Matthew 25:14-30)

There is a similar scenario: there is a going, there is an absence, and there is a return. The master, distributing the talents to his servants, said, Use them till I come back. Then he leaves them, and they do different things with the talents that he gave them. When he returns, there is a reckoning, there is a judgment, there is an evaluation, there is an assessment.

What about the plain teaching of Jesus, the straightforward statements that he makes? Over twenty-one times Jesus makes clear statements concerning his second coming. The nearer he gets to his crucifixion, the more clearly he speaks of his return in glory.

In Matthew 26:64, he said, 'I say to all of you: In the future, you will see the Son of Man [his favourite title for himself] sitting at the right hand of the Mighty One [that is, God] and coming on the clouds of heaven.' And in Luke 21:27 he said, 'At that time they will see the Son of Man coming in a cloud with power and great glory.'

Maybe you have been recently at a funeral service and heard the words that Jesus spoke in the upper room when giving a bedrock promise to his disciples: 'If I go and prepare a place for you, I will come back' (John 14:3). General Douglas McArthur said when he left the Philippines, after it was invaded by the Japanese: 'I will return.' Here is Jesus Christ's great word to his people: 'I will come back and take you to be with me that you also may be where I am.'

One simply cannot hail Jesus as a great teacher and evade his teaching about his second coming. Either Jesus is a mad man, or he is a bad man, or he is God, and said the truth when he spoke these words.

Jesus as Saviour

What did he come to do? Did he simply come to offer us a moral code? No! He came to offer us eternal life.

He said to the grieving sisters at the grave of Lazarus: 'I am the resurrection and the life. He who believes in me will live, even though he dies' (John 11:25). What did he mean by that? Live in the memories of those who loved them? No! Jesus says: 'I will raise them up on the last day.'

In other words, we have yet to see the consummation of the saving work of Jesus Christ. If the work of Jesus Christ in salvation is simply to save our souls and give us a kind of spiritual, ethereal experience of eternal life, then quite frankly, what he offers is no better than what can be experienced in other religions. Our confidence in Jesus Christ is of the resurrection of the body on the last day, of the renovation of the universe at the end of the age, of the complete putting-together of that which is falling apart. Environmentally, universally, a reversal of things as they are.

There was a time when it seemed as if Jesus' words about his full and final salvation were empty. His disciples skulked in an upper room behind closed doors, and his body lay in a Jewish tomb. But on that first Easter morning when they found the tomb empty, when they found the grave clothes undisturbed, when they met the Lord Jesus in person in various places, at various times, they became convinced not only of his resurrection, but of everything else about him — his claims about the salvation he gives were true.

The writer to the Hebrews correctly understands the work of salvation when he says about the Lord Jesus that he came the first time to deal with sin, to bear sin in his own body on the cross. And he will come a second time to bring salvation to those who believe in him (Hebrews 9:28).

So our Christian certainty rests then on the word of God the Father, in prophecy and in history; it rests upon the work of the Son as teacher and as Saviour; and thirdly, on the witness and the testimony of God the Holy Spirit.

The Witness of God the Holy Spirit
There are two things to say about the witness of God the Spirit.

First of all, it is an *apostolic* witness. Do you remember when Jesus was in the upper room with his eleven apostles (Judas had left)? Jesus promised to those eleven that they would receive a special ministry of the Holy Spirit. This is what the Holy Spirit would do for them: 'The Counsellor, the Holy Spirit, whom the Father will send in my name, will teach you all things and will remind you of everything I have said to you' (John 14:26); 'When he, the Spirit of truth, comes, he will guide

you into all truth' (John 16:13). He will remind
them of everything Jesus said to them. He will
guide them into all truth. He will tell them what is
yet to come.

The promise of Jesus that the Holy Spirit would
come upon them was fulfilled on the day of
Pentecost, surrounded by miraculous signs that
were indisputable. Languages that were unlearned
were spoken, and could be understood by the
milling throngs in Jerusalem; there was the sound
of a strong wind, the fire: all evidences of the
Spirit's arrival. It was the reversal of the tragedy of
Babel when everybody was given a different language and could not understand one another. A
reversal of that, because on the day of Pentecost
everybody heard in their own tongue the mighty
works of God.

On the day of Pentecost the Spirit began the
work of reminding the apostles of all Jesus had said
and done, of leading them into a supplementation
of that, and giving them fresh insights into the
truth, telling them about things to come. And in the
historical parts of our New Testament, we have a
record of what Jesus said and did. In the doctrinal
parts of it, the letters, we have a record of the
teaching of the Holy Spirit, the leading into all the
truth by the Spirit; and in the prophetic sections we
have the outline of things to come.

It does not matter whether we read Matthew,

Mark, Luke, John, Paul, James, the writer to the Hebrews, or Jude, all of them bear witness to the second coming of Jesus. Here are some examples:

Paul: 'For the Lord himself will come down from heaven, with a loud command, with the voice of the archangel and with the trumpet call of God' (1 Thessalonians 4:16).

Peter: 'But the day of the Lord will come like a thief. The heavens will disappear with a roar; the elements will be destroyed by fire, and the earth and everything in it will be laid bare' (2 Peter 3:10).

James: 'Be patient, then, brothers, until the Lord's coming ... be patient and stand firm, because the Lord's coming is near' (James 5:7,8).

John: 'Dear friends, now we are children of God, and what we will be has not yet been made known. But we know that when he appears, we shall be like him, for we shall see him as he is' (1 John 3:2).

Hebrews: 'He [Christ] will appear a second time, not to bear sin, but to bring salvation to those who are waiting for him' (Hebrews 9:28).

Jude: 'See, the Lord is coming with thousands upon thousands of his holy ones to judge everyone, and to convict all the ungodly of all the ungodly acts they have done in the ungodly way, and of all the harsh words ungodly sinners have spoken against him' (verses 14-15).

These early Christians, who had seen the Lord Jesus alive from the dead, spoke of the second coming of Jesus. The witness of the Spirit is an apostolic witness found in Scripture.

But this witness of the Holy Spirit is not only apostolic, it is *catholic*. This word 'catholic' means universal. When we say the witness of the Spirit to the coming of Jesus is catholic, we are saying it is a witness that is given to all the people of God, throughout all the ages, and today. All Christians have this living hope in the return of Jesus Christ.

Paul in Romans 8:23 speaks of the Holy Spirit as the 'first fruits' who guarantees that God is going to continue working in our lives, and who increases our anticipation of the day of Christ's return. In Ephesians 1:13-14, Paul uses a word for the Holy Spirit which means a pledge, a guarantee of good things to come, the down-payment of what is yet in store for us.

So one of the ministries of the Spirit in the life of the individual Christian has been to stir up in their hearts this hope in the returning Lord. You will find evidence for that if you look at church history and at the church of Jesus Christ today. There is no major creed or major confession of the Christian church that does not bear testimony to the second coming of Jesus Christ.

Read the Nicene Creed or the Athanasian Creed, or the Apostles' Creed that is recited in Orthodox, Roman, Anglican and Non-Conformist churches across the world today: From heaven 'he shall come to judge the living and the dead'. It is in the Augsburg confession of the Lutheran church. It is in the Thirty-Nine Articles of the Anglican church — number 4 of the Articles reads: 'He ascended into heaven and there he sits until he returns to judge all men in the last day.' It is contained in every significant Catholic, Baptist, Pentecostal and Presbyterian statement of faith. Jesus Christ shall return. It is one of the most catholic, most universal of doctrines held by the people of God in every age and in every place.

Attend a Christian funeral service – it matters not the denominational badge or labels – you will discover that they bury their Christian dead in sure and certain hope of the resurrection on the last day. Come to a Christian communion service, whether it is called Eucharist or Lord's Supper or Communion. At that service believers eat and drink the tokens of their Lord's dying – till he come. In some churches of our day, at the Communion service there will be reiterated the three-fold affirmation that lies at the very heart of the mystery of our religion: Christ has died, Christ is risen, Christ will come again.

The certainty of Jesus Christ's coming is based upon these three great foundations for the Christian believer: the word of God the Father, expressed in prophecy, confirmed in history; the work of God the Son as the great teacher who spoke clearly of his coming again and a Saviour who saw it as the confirmation of that which he had begun by his cross and by his resurrection; the witness of God the Holy Spirit which is both apostolic - found in Scripture - and catholic, the universal hope of every Christian and every Christian church.

'Do you know where you are going?' Thomas Huxley asked his taxi-driver. 'No, but I'm getting there as fast as I can!' The world's philosophy has been stated to be this: to travel hopefully is better than to arrive.

'Do you know where you are going?' the world asks the Christian church. In the midst of all the confusion of our day, the Christian says: Yes. The world hopes for the best, but Jesus Christ offers the best hope for the world.

Throughout the centuries there have been two words that Christians have never felt free to translate into their native, indigenous languages: one is Aramaic, 'Maranatha'; the other is Hebrew, 'Hallelujah'. One is a prayer and an assertion: 'Our Lord come'. The other means, 'Praise the Lord'.

These two words constitute the strongest, firmest, best message that we can say to our disintegrating world today. They constitute the most fundamental statement that I can say into your private world, which may equally well be disintegrating: Maranatha, Hallelujah! Our Lord come! Praise the Lord!

3

ITS MANNER

Wrong focusing by the Church
Christ's second coming will be personal
Christ's second coming will be visible
Christ's second coming will be glorious
Christ's second coming will be decisive
Christ's second coming will be sudden
What is the relevance of the Second Coming?

3

A dramatic shift of thought has taken place in the Western world during the last fifty years. The result is a greater emphasis on personal relevance, on the meaning of experience in my life now, with a disinterest both in history and in the future.

Wrong focusing by the Church

Even when we look at Christianity and the Christian church we discover that Christian teaching has been pervaded by this prevailing climate. In popular teaching the stress is on what Jesus can do for me now, rather than in what Jesus has done for me in the past on the cross, and on what Jesus will do in the future when he comes again. Very often this comes out in what we pray about.

Often before a service Christians will pray that God would see people where they are and meet their need in the service. In the past, the great concern that would have consumed people as they prayed about a service of Christian worship would

have been that God would be exalted, that he would
be glorified.

You can express the change that has taken
place, I suppose, in a couple of popular slogans in
the evangelical world: what Christianity is about,
we are told, is not about pie-in-the-sky-when-you-
die, it is about steak-on-the-plate-while-you-wait!
And that shift of emphasis from understanding that
all of life is lived in the perspective of the end of the
age, affects the way we live here and now.

It was Martyn Lloyd-Jones who said that he
began his public ministry by preaching on the text:
'Here we have no continuing city.' He was asked
what he would preach on if he knew this would be
his last opportunity to preach the Word. He said,
'To preach on the very same text.'

As Christians we are to remember that here we
have no continuing city, that we are on the move.
We are people on a journey, we are heading
forward towards the climax which God has prepared for those that love him.

Paul, writing in 1 Corinthians 15:19, addresses
this modern mentality of saying that really what it
is all about is what Jesus can do for you here and now.
He says this: 'If only for this life we have hope in
Christ, we are to be pitied more than all men'; that
is, if all there is to Christianity is what Jesus can do
for you here and now, wonderful though that may
be, then, says Paul, we are to be pitied!

But the hope of Christ's return at the end of history is the logical and necessary outcome of our faith. What God has already done for man's salvation in the life, death and resurrection of Jesus Christ, has a glorious future completion in the mind of God. For if you remove the return of Jesus from the plan of salvation, you will discover it to be a plan that has a beginning without an end. Emil Brunner put it like this:

> Faith in Jesus, without the expectation of his return, is a cheque that has never been cashed, a promise that is not made in dead earnest. A faith in Christ without the expectation of a return is like a flight of stairs that leads nowhere, but ends in the void.

The second coming of Jesus is not some minor theme in the Bible's teaching; it is seen to be the proper and appropriate climax to the work of Christ begun at his incarnation. It is dealt with over 1,800 times in the Bible. There are 300 references to it in the New Testament, an average of one reference to every thirteen verses. In this chapter we will look at the question of how Jesus will return. What will be the manner of his coming?

A lesson in Greek

By way of introduction, there are three words used in the Greek New Testament to describe the return of the Lord Jesus Christ.

The first word is *parousia*, meaning coming, or arrival, or presence. Sometimes it is used in a very ordinary sense in the New Testament. For example, when Paul is writing about the coming of a man called Stephanos, he uses this word. He also uses this word when he describes his own coming and his arrival and his staying with a church to whom he is writing. I think the best way of understanding those two ideas of a coming and a presence together, is to use the word 'arrival'. For the coming of the Lord Jesus is an expected event, and when it happens there will be the Lord's personal arrival and his personal presence with his people.

The second word is *epiphany*, which is linked in a number of references with *parousia* to describe Christ's return (cf. 2 Thessalonians 2:8; 1 John 2:28, 3:2). But most often this word *epiphany* emphasises the glorious aspect of the return of Jesus. In Titus 2:13, Paul wrote that 'we wait for the blessed hope — the glorious *epiphany* of our great God and Saviour, Jesus Christ'.

In the Greek world this word was used to describe the solemn, splendid entrance of a ruler or a prince. If you can imagine something splendid, that is an *epiphany*.

The third word used is *apocalypse*, which means to reveal or to unveil. It conveys the idea 'to make known', of making visible something that has been invisible. It carries the idea of drawing back a curtain, so that what is already there behind the curtain may be seen.

At a stage play before the curtains are pulled back, the actors have been setting themselves up for the first scene. When the curtain is drawn back, you see what has been there but hidden. The return of Jesus will be the pulling aside of the curtain, so that we see the eternal world that is there all the time, but hidden to our eyes.

So if we put those three words together, we can say that the manner of Jesus' appearing will be an arrival, an entrance and an unveiling.

Some years ago we as a family went to Bournemouth for a holiday. It was the time of the wedding of Prince Charles and Lady Diana, and we were very interested in watching it on television. Although it was a brilliantly sunny day, about eighty degrees, we stayed in as dutiful citizens to watch this great event on television.

As we watched, the commentator described what was happening inside the cathedral, informing the viewing audience that so-and-so had arrived and where they were sitting. Then the cameras switched to Buckingham Palace, and we saw the horse-drawn coach as it left the palace and swept down the Mall towards the cathedral.

As the carriage passed the various locations along the route where the television cameras were set up, there was all kind of debate among the commentators as to what Diana's dress was like, because they had very few glimpses of it. They could see her smiling and so forth but there was a great deal of excitement being generated about the dress. Incredible to me, but there you are!

Eventually she arrived in front of the cathedral and as the door opened and she stepped down, there was a flurry of trumpets from inside the cathedral. She had arrived, she was making a grand entrance, and there was a revelation of the dress. We saw her in all the splendour and beauty of a bride dressed for her wedding.

In that event we see those three ideas of arrival, a grand splendid entrance and a revelation of something that was hidden but is now disclosed for all to see. They are the ideas behind these three words that are used in the Greek New Testament to describe the Lord's return. Flowing from that, I will make five propositions concerning the Second Coming.

1. Christ's second coming will be personal

Now this aspect of the second coming of Jesus can raise a problem in some minds. Does not the Bible teach that the Lord Jesus is never absent from his

people? Surely the Lord is with his people wherever they are? Right across the world, wherever
God's people are gathered together, Jesus is present.
Jesus promised that when two or three are gathered
together in his name he would be in their midst.
Just before he ascended back to heaven, and to
encourage his disciples to fulfil his Great Commis-
sion, he promised: 'Surely I am with you always,
to the very end of the age' (Matthew 28:20).

The answer to this apparent contradiction is
found in the Lord's teaching in the upper room
(John 13-17). Jesus informed his disciples that he
would send the Holy Spirit to indwell them, to be
beside them, supporting them, counselling them.
The Spirit would be the perpetual presence of Jesus
with all of his people, wherever they are, in whatever circumstances they find themselves. That is
why Christian people can testify to the reality of
the presence of the Lord Jesus, both individually in
their own lives and corporately as they gather for
worship, witness and fellowship.

Paul discovered this in his own experience. It
meant the living reality of the presence of God in
his life, by which he was encouraged to believe that
he was a child of God and able to say, 'Abba,
Father'. But he further says in Romans 8:23-24
that we who 'have the firstfruits of the Spirit, groan
inwardly as we wait eagerly for our adoption as
sons, the redemption of our bodies. For in this hope

we were saved'. In other words, says Paul, the reality of the experience of the Lord Jesus in my life right now, doesn't diminish the longing I have to see him in his glory, to see him personally when he comes again. The fact is that however real their experience of the Lord Jesus Christ now, it has never diminished the Christian's longing for the Lord's return.

In John 14:3 Jesus gives the ultimate promise when he says to his disciples: 'I will come back and take you to be with me that you also may be where I am', and he underlines this by saying that it is a promise not only of the Son but also of the Father to his people (14:1).

In the record of the ascension of the Lord Jesus Christ into heaven, recorded in Acts 1:1-11, the two men dressed in white say to the gazing disciples: 'Men of Galilee, why do you stand here looking into the sky? This same Jesus [notice that, underline it in your Bible] who has been taken from you into heaven, will come back in the same way you have seen him go into heaven.'

Christ's second coming will be personal.

2. Christ's second coming will be visible

Jehovah's Witnesses claim that Jesus Christ returned in 1914 in an invisible way. That runs contrary to everything the New Testament teaches about the Lord Jesus' return.

Take two of the words we looked at: the word *epiphany* (an entrance) and the word *apocalypse* (a revelation of something). Both of them convey the idea of something that is public. In Titus 2:11-13, for example, you have *epiphany* used in its verbal form to describe the Lord Jesus' first coming: 'The grace of God has appeared to all men'. In other words, Jesus arrived and he was displayed in public, especially at his baptism. He came to be the manifestation of the grace of God here on planet Earth. People could see him.

Then Paul uses the same word in its noun form when he refers to the glorious *appearing* of our great God and Saviour Jesus Christ. In other words, what Paul is saying is that the second coming of Jesus will be as visible as his first coming.

In fact the word *apocalypse* suggests that the second coming will make clear to everyone what the first coming was all about. It will be a revelation, an unveiling of the true nature of Christ's person. In Revelation 1:9, John writes: 'Look, he is coming with clouds and every eye will see him.' There will be nobody anywhere in the universe who will not see Jesus when he comes.

In order to understand this we need to evacuate our minds of the kind of spatial, temporal limitations that we are bound to in our thinking. We should think of the appearance of Jesus in more dimensional terms, instead of spatial terms. Not so much in terms of Jesus coming down in a cloud, visible only to a group of people in a particular location, but Jesus appearing dimensionally, a new dimension that we haven't yet understood or perceived, a barrier through which we have not yet broken. Jesus visually appearing to the world, publicly.

His coming will be visible.

3. Christ's second coming will be glorious

When Jesus came the first time, he fulfilled the prophecy of Isaiah 42: 'He will not shout or cry out, or raise his voice in the streets' (verse 2). Isaiah was saying that it would be a low-key coming.

That's what it was like. Born in obscurity, raised away from the public eye, living his life, as it were, out of the spotlight. Indeed, during his three-year ministry, Jesus repeatedly commanded his hearers and those that he healed, not to make him known. Isn't that amazing? Even at such high points in his ministry such as Peter's confession, 'You are the Christ, the Son of God', or his Transfiguration, when Moses and Elijah appeared with him and God said 'This is my Beloved Son, hear him', Jesus told his disciples to keep quiet about it.

Even though today Jesus Christ is proclaimed to the world as the Messiah, the Lord, the Son of God, only when he returns will his true glory be manifested for all to see.

There are books, written especially towards the end of the last century, which suggest that by the preaching of the gospel we could reproduce something of the glory of Christ in the world, simply by the numbers of people who are being converted. While I am sure that would bring great glory to Jesus, the fullness of the manifestation of Jesus' glory awaits the day when he will come in person to be seen, universally, irresistibly and visibly. At his return, gone forever will be the obscurity of the hiddenness and the apparent weakness. Listen to Jesus' words in Matthew 24:27: 'For as lightning that comes from the east is visible even in the west, so will be the coming of the Son of Man.'

In the same chapter Jesus said : 'If anyone tells you, "There he is, out in the desert," do not go out; or, "Here he is in the inner rooms," do not believe it' (verse 26). There was an article in a newspaper a few years ago saying that Jesus Christ had arrived and was living in obscurity somewhere in Belgium. Bible-believing Christians would not believe that nonsense; the coming of the Son of Man will be a public spectacle of his glory.

Paul said that the Lord Jesus will come down from heaven, with a loud command (1 Thessalonians 4:16). It is all noise, it is trumpets blowing, it is the voice of the archangel, it is the shaking of the universe, it is everything to draw attention to the glory of the Lord Jesus, as he descends from heaven. Jesus, who emptied himself to become the Servant, and then humbled himself even to the death of the cross, is to return as the glorious Conqueror, the Judge of all, the Redeemer of his people, the King of kings, the Lord of lords. Every knee shall bow before him.

His coming will be glorious.

4. Christ's second coming will be decisive

In 1 Corinthians 15:24, Paul, writing about the coming of Jesus, said: 'Then the end will come.' At the return of Jesus Christ the long march of the ages will come to an end. The scheming and plotting of men will finish. The last page of the history books will be written. The last act of the human drama will be played out. The curtain will fall on the stage of time.

Paul, writing in Ephesians 1 about the scenario of God's redemption, speaks about God's plans being formulated in his mind before the beginning of the world; how he chose a people, and planned the way of their salvation which he determined to achieve through the work of Christ upon the Cross. Then Paul reaches a climactic moment when he says that God's eternal purpose is to head up everything under Jesus Christ.

The whole of history is moving forward to that

dramatic event of the coming again of Jesus in glory. That is where our world is heading. It is an event written into every human diary, including that of politicians, by God. Whatever other events in history are negotiable because of circumstances, here is one event that is non-negotiable. Jesus is going to come and that will be the end of history as we know it.

Back in 1860 a French scientist called Pierre Berchert said that inside of 100 years of physical and chemical science, man will know what the atom is. It is my belief that when science reaches that stage, God will come down to earth with his big ring of keys and will say to humanity, 'Gentlemen, it is closing time.' It will be the end point of human history.

The second coming of Jesus will be decisive.

5. Christ's second coming will be sudden
Jesus said: 'The Son of Man will come at an hour when you do not expect him' (Matthew 25:44).

To emphasise this aspect of his teaching, Jesus used several illustrations. He said his return would be similar to the lightning that flashes from the east to the west. He taught that his coming would be like a 'thief in the night'. He referred to the flood of Noah's day. As it was in the days of Noah so shall it be when I return, said Jesus.

What were people doing when the flood came?

They were eating and drinking, they were marrying and giving in marriage. In other words what they were doing was nothing unusual. They were carrying on the normal, legitimate functions of life, and in the normal course of things they were making normal assumptions about tomorrow and next week and next year, when the flood came and overwhelmed them.

It will be a day like any other day when Jesus Christ comes. You will wake up in the morning and you will swing your legs out of bed and you will maybe wash yourself. You may be feeling particularly virtuous so you will bring your wife or husband breakfast in bed. Then you will go to work, or do whatever is your normal day's activities. Perhaps you will make some appointments for the following weeks, when suddenly, in the normal course of events, Jesus will come. That is the teaching. Just as it was in the days of Noah, so will it be in the days of the coming of the Son of Man.

C. S. Lewis, the great Oxford writer, commented on this. He said that the doctrine of the Second Coming may be to some people intolerably frustrating. Perhaps they were going to get married next month; perhaps they were going to get a raise next week. Some may be on the verge of a great scientific discovery. Others may be maturing great social and political reforms. But, then of all moments, Jesus will come again.

Jesus Christ is coming personally, visibly, gloriously, decisively, suddenly.

What is the relevance of the Second Coming?

To those who are not committed Christians — why is it that this day has not yet arrived? Peter tells us: 'God is patient with you, not wanting anyone to perish, but everyone to come to repentance' (2 Peter 3:9). God is giving non-Christians time to turn from a life of sin and begin to follow Jesus.

He has given warnings. God speaks to men and women through the cataclysmic events that affect our world; the earthquakes, the famines, the football violence and the destructiveness of man in his wars: Repent, turn to me! The fact is that a day is coming when there will be no time to get ready, to stop and think, to get right with God. That is why Paul says: 'Now is the accepted time, now is the day of salvation' (2 Corinthians 6:12).

What about those who are committed Christians? Sometimes this doctrine has been trivialised. I remember the abject fear with which I went for the very first time into a cinema, because it had been said to me, What would you do if Jesus came back and found you in the cinema? But I sat right through Dr. Zhivago, and he didn't! And I breathed a sigh of relief. There is a sense in which that kind of thing has trivialised the coming again of the Lord Jesus.

Dr. G. Campbell-Morgan, the great Bible teacher, once wrote: 'I never lay my head on the pillow without thinking that perhaps before I awake the final morning may have dawned. I never begin my work without thinking that he may interrupt it, and begin his work.'

What do we do with the second coming of Jesus? Do we do as some Christians in the last and present centuries have done? Sell our homes, give up our jobs and camp on a mountain top, or in some remote spot, and wait for the millennial day to dawn? No, that is not what the Bible says!

What we are meant to do is this. When we wake up in the morning, we are to place ourselves, as we should do each day, into the hands of God, and live each day and make each decision and do each duty, living so as to be unashamed if at any moment Jesus Christ would interrupt us.

John Wesley was once asked: 'Mr. Wesley, what would you do if you knew that Jesus was coming again tomorrow afternoon at five o'clock?'

He took out his diary and then said: 'Well, I would retire to bed at ten o'clock this evening as I usually do. I would sing a psalm of praise to the Lord Jesus and then go to sleep. I would wake tomorrow morning and read a chapter from Isaiah, that I am reading through at the moment. I would then travel to Mrs.— to have breakfast there and then I would speak to a group of miners early in the morning. I would then proceed to have dinner with some people at lunch-time.' And so he went through the day, and then said, 'At five o'clock I would be able to shut my diary and welcome my Jesus back.'

Do we organise our lives as Martin Luther did who lived as if Jesus Christ died yesterday, rose today, and was coming again tomorrow? Are we in a state of readiness? Should Jesus come just now, would we gladly rise to meet him, or shrink from him in shame? This is the issue. It is not an issue of fear, but it is an issue of godliness.

4

ITS PURPOSE

Christ is coming to ransom his church
Christ is coming to resurrect the dead
Christ is coming to review our works
Christ is coming to renew the cosmos
Christ is coming to reign as Lord

4

We have looked already at the certainty of Christ's return, rooted as it is in God's Word. He has given us further assurance in Christ's work as teacher and as Saviour, and in the Holy Spirit's witness, both apostolic (to be found in Scripture) and catholic (the universal belief of the Church). Then we looked at the manner of Christ's return — it is personal, visible, glorious, decisive and sudden. And now in this chapter we are going to look at the purpose of Christ's return.

Why is Jesus Christ returning? There are at least five things that the Bible identifies as reasons for the return of the Lord Jesus.

1. Christ is coming to ransom his church

As you read the New Testament you discover that in a number of places the return of Jesus is linked very closely to the deliverance or the rescue of the people of God.

This world is described in the Bible as a place

of 'testing', of temptation, of trouble, for the followers of Christ. There are also several passages which teach that there will be particular difficulties for believers immediately prior to the coming again of Jesus. And therefore the coming of the Lord Jesus is related directly to delivering them from this sphere of trouble, testing and tribulation.

Scripture also relates the coming of Jesus to the anxiety that Christian people very often have about being separated from their loved ones. Where are the dead who die in the Lord? is a question that is addressed in the New Testament. And so we find the Bible saying that the Lord by his coming will deliver his people, will ransom them from their enemies, will rescue them from their trouble, and will reunite them with each other, and with himself.

Some of the great passages, such as 1 Corinthians 15 and 1 Thessalonians 4, speak in these terms. Christians who have died are described as those who are asleep in Christ. This description shows that they are not unconscious but that they are waiting for something: the Day of Resurrection, when the dead in Christ shall rise from the dead and, together with those Christians then alive, be caught up to meet the Lord in the air.

In the previous chapter, we saw that the Lord will return in splendour, manifesting the power and glory which was hidden from men. The Lord's very first movement of that dramatic sweep into world history will be to catch up his people, and gather them together. There will be a reunion, not only of Christians one with the other, but of Christians with the Lord, as they gather together around the one whose coming they anticipated. That really is the focal point of Christian hope. That is the point, to which as Christians, as the people of God, we are moving. It is to be ransomed from this sphere of temptation, trouble and sin; to be redeemed and reunited with those who have died in the Lord and are now with him.

As I was walking to church one morning, I started to sing — not out loud you understand! In my mind I recalled the words of a hymn that my mother used to sing to me. In her young days she used to go to the Tent Hall in Glasgow where there was a Scottish evangelist called Jock Troup and one of his favourite songs was a song about the coming again of Jesus:

> You have heard of little Moses in the bulrush,
> You have heard of fearless David and his sling,
> You have heard the story told of dreaming Joseph,
> And of Jonah and the Whale we often sing.
>
> There are many many others in the Bible;
> I should like to meet them all, I do declare.
> By and by the Lord will surely let us meet them
> At that meeting in the air.

There is going to be a meeting in the air
In the sweet, sweet by-and-by.

They are old-fashioned words but they express the idea not only of meeting with the Lord, but of meeting with the Lord's people on that day.

Paul writing in 1 Thessalonians 4 ends his statement of the Lord's return by saying 'And so we will be with the Lord for ever.' The image of the bride waiting for her bridegroom pictures the anticipation and the expectation and the thrill of reunion with the Lord whom we love.

That is wrapped up in this promise of the Lord's return. He is coming to ransom his people.

2. Christ is coming to resurrect the dead
The resurrection of the dead is hinted at in the Old Testament Scriptures.

Job says in a great passage: 'After my skin has been destroyed, yet in my flesh I will see God' (Job 19:26). Isaiah writes: 'Your dead will live; their bodies will rise' (26:19). And Daniel says: 'Multitudes who sleep in the dust of the earth will awake: some to everlasting life, others to shame and everlasting contempt' (Daniel 12:2).

These clear references in the Old Testament to the resurrection on the last day were enough to give orthodox Judaism a very firm understanding that this was their hope and their confidence. But it is with the arrival of the Lord Jesus, bringing life and immortality to light in the gospel, that the focus on the resurrection becomes even clearer for us.

Think of Jesus' words in John 5: 28,29: 'All who are in their graves will hear his [the Son of Man's] voice and come out — those who have done good will rise to live, and those who have done evil will rise to be condemned.' Or Paul, in 1 Corinthians 15:

> We will not all sleep, but we will all be changed — in a flash, in the twinkling of an eye, at the last trumpet. For the trumpet will sound, the dead will be raised imperishable, and we will be changed. For the perishable must clothe itself with the imperishable, and the mortal with immortality. When the perishable has been clothed with the imperishable, and the mortal with immortality, then the saying that is written will come true: 'Death has been swallowed up in victory' (verses 51-54).

We need to understand the background into which that kind of language was spoken. These Christian people lived in a climate of thought where the idea was that the body was inherently evil. Salvation, to have any meaningful relevance, must mean the salvation of the spirit or soul. The body was regarded as limiting man's expression of real existence and real freedom. But, contrary to that view, the Bible teaches that God created man body and spirit; man is not complete apart from the body. The Scriptures further teach that because Christ rose from the dead, all Christians shall rise with glorified bodies like his glorified body.

That is important for us to grasp. The almost exclusive preoccupation of evangelistic preaching today seems to be the redemption of the soul here and now. But complete redemption must include the soul and the body, the whole person redeemed and raised up on the final day.

There are two questions that are often asked about the resurrection. First, *what is the scope of the resurrection*? In answer to that question, we emphasise that it will include both believers and unbelievers. I have already quoted a couple of references which so suggest. Paul also says in Acts 24:15: 'There will be a resurrection of both the righteous and the wicked.' Both will be raised on that day.

Secondly, *what about the nature of the resurrection body*? The Bible tells us very little but gives a few hints: for example, it will be like Christ's risen body (Philippians 3:21); it will be a body devoid of corruption, weakness, dishonour, sickness and death (1 Corinthians 15:42-4). It will go f beyond our present limited experience.

et there are two things we can say about the of the resurrection body. Firstly, it will be

suited for a very different level of existence. It will
be the life of the new order, an existence without
the limitations brought about by the Fall and sin. It
will be a body with different faculties, enlarged
abilities and different properties altogether. We
shall be changed, Paul says in 1 Corinthians 15.
Flesh and blood as we know it cannot inherit the
kingdom of God, nor does the perishable inherit
the imperishable.

Secondly, Paul relates our existence now with
our existence then by using the analogy of a seed
that is planted and then grows into a beautiful
flower or productive crop. In this illustration, Paul
pictures our present body as that uninviting, ugly
little seed, which is sowed in death but blossoms
into new life in the resurrection. Our present
bodies are the seed of that resurrection. So not only
will it be a different level of existence, but there
will be some degree of continuity between life now
and life then. Although we shall be changed, we
will certainly recognise one another in the resurrection.

Christ is coming to resurrect the dead.

3. Christ is coming to review our works
Paul writing to Timothy speaks of Jesus 'who will
judge the living and the dead' (2 Timothy 4:1).

There is a sense in which we can say that people
are judged already. Their response to the gospel

message of Jesus Christ in a sense declares their judgment. 'This is the verdict: Light has come into the world, but men loved darkness instead of light because their deeds were evil' (John 3:19).

Nevertheless, the Bible says that a day is coming when God will display to the universe his sovereignty over everything and everyone, by calling everybody, great and small, rich and poor, Christian and non-Christian, to render account before him.

In Acts 17:31, Paul said that God 'has set a day when he will judge the world with justice by the man he has appointed.' John, in the book of Revelation, sees a great white throne from which judgment is executed on the mass of humanity gathered around it (20:11-13). Christ is the one to whom God has given all authority in heaven and earth. The Father has appointed him as the Judge of all mankind.

Who will be judged?

The Bible says the fallen angels, including the devil, will be judged on that day (Jude 6; 2 Peter 2:4). All human beings will be judged. Every human being who ever lived will be judged on that day. Believers will be judged. We can't avoid that. Paul says, writing to the Corinthians: 'We must all appear before the judgment seat of Christ' (2 Corinthians 5:10).

What will be judged?

'We must all appear before the judgment seat of

Christ that each one may receive what is due to him for the things done while in the body, whether good or bad' (1 Corinthians 5:10).

What are those things?

From various scriptures we discover that they include deeds; they include words — every idle word will have to be accounted for; they include thoughts — the thoughts and intents of the heart will be laid bare on that day. Our deeds, our words, our thoughts will be exposed before the Judge. Sinners will be judged on the basis of sin, for the standard of judgment will be the revealed will of God.

How have people responded and behaved in relation to the light they have had? It could be the light of nature or the light of conscience or the light of Scripture. Paul says that everybody will be demonstrated to have been without excuse (Romans 3:9-20). But it seems that those who are condemned will suffer degrees of punishment. Because the grace of God has come in Christ Jesus, the judgment of God will be more severe upon those who reject the gospel. Jesus said it would be more tolerable for Sodom and Gomorrah on the Day of Judgment, than for the city that rejects the message of the kingdom of God (cf. Luke 10:13-14).

If for the unbeliever the judgment is to be a moment of condemnation, for the Christian the judgment will be a moment of vindication. Before the watching universe, not only will their sins be exposed, but they are proclaimed to have been covered and forgiven by the blood of the Lord Jesus. That foundation remains inviolable; there is nothing that can bring the child of God under condemnation on the Judgment Day. There is now no condemnation for those who are in Christ Jesus.

But Paul asks the question in 1 Corinthians 3: How have we built on the foundation? How have we as Christian people used our time, our talents, our opportunities, our responsibilities and our duties? Do you know that it is possible for all of our works as believers to be consumed by the fire of the coming of the Lord? It is possible to suffer loss; to be saved, but 'as one escaping through the flames' (1 Corinthians 3:15).

Do you know that it is conceivable for believers to be ashamed at Jesus' coming? Ashamed! My brothers and sisters in Christ Jesus, it is an awful thing to fall into the hands of an angry God!

Just as there are degrees of punishment for the condemned, so there are degrees of reward for the justified. The key for those who know the Lord is to be found faithful when he appears. We will look more at this in the next chapter when we consider the challenge of his coming.

So sinners will be judged on the basis of sin, but saints will be judged on the basis of stewardship.

4. Christ is coming to renew the cosmos

We can get the impression from certain hymns, and it is certainly the caricature that the world paints, that the glorified believer will spend eternity floating in an ethereal heaven somewhere off in space, strumming harps. I can't think of anything more boring than sitting on a cloud somewhere strumming a harp — I can't even play a harp!

But that is not the Bible's teaching. What it reveals is that the return of Jesus will be accompanied by cosmic phenomena affecting not just the planet but the universe.

Peter says so in the third chapter of his second letter:

> 'The day of the Lord will come like a thief. The heavens will disappear with a roar; the elements will be destroyed by fire, and the earth and everything in it will be laid bare. ... That day will bring about the destruction of the heavens by fire, and the elements will melt in the heat. But in keeping with his promise we are looking forward to a new heaven and a new earth, the home of righteousness' (verses 10, 12-13).

Paul in Romans 8 describes the present condition of creation, disturbed by the ravages of sin's effects — pollution, environmental damage and many other things. He says the whole creation groans 'as in the pains of childbirth' at this present time, waiting for the moment when the sons of God will be revealed. Why? Because it will be 'liberated from its bondage to decay and brought into the glorious freedom of the children of God' (verses 19-22).

What is Paul saying there, in his theological language? He is saying this, the return of Jesus Christ is going to see the liberation of the universe, locked in as it is to the effects of sin, to the entropy of sin and the disintegration of sin. There will be a renewal of all things (Matthew 19:28), a new heaven and a new earth, when nature will be at peace with itself, when the barrier between God's presence in heaven and our life on earth will be removed and heaven will come on earth.

Believers are destined not to live in heaven, but to live and work and serve in a renovated universe, a place where all the things that are offered in the gospel and indicated by the miracles and ministry of Jesus become a reality. Where is there perfect health, perfect healing, perfect harmony and perfect happiness? In the new heaven and new earth.

Just as there is continuity between the body we have now and the resurrection body, there will be continuity between life here and life there. There will be trees and rivers, technology and science, adventure and exploration. Mankind will fulfil the mandate given to them in creation to explore, expand and develop the universe that God has made, to subdue it as men and women liberated from the greed and corruption of indwelling sin.

Jesus is coming to renew the cosmos.

5. Christ is coming to reign as Lord

In 1 Corinthians 15:24 Paul refers to the end: 'Then the end will come'. When is this?

He has already said it is connected to the coming of the Lord (verse 23), when he has destroyed all dominion, authority and power, for he says: 'He must reign until he has put all his enemies under his feet' (verse 25).

Paul states that the coming again of the Lord Jesus will bring about the conclusion of the process by which all the enemies of God have been systematically and successively overthrown throughout the centuries. The effects of sin will be reversed. Satan will finally be destroyed. God's original purposes in creation will come to pass, and all the promise and the achievement of the Lord's first coming will be fulfilled in his second coming.

There is a direct relation — we must never lose the link between his first and his second comings; the second coming will be the final act in the drama of redemption. Do you see this movement as you read the Bible? What a climactic statement is found in Revelation 11:15: 'The kingdom of the world has become the kingdom of our Lord and of his Christ, and he will reign for ever and ever'!

At the coronation of Queen Elizabeth II in 1953, there was an unforgettable moment when the Archbishop of Canterbury, Dr. Geoffrey Fisher, extended the crown to Her Majesty in the historic prayer book service, and said these words: 'I give thee, O sovereign lady, this crown to wear, until he who reserves the right to wear it, shall return.'

Jesus is coming to assume his rightful prerogatives. Paul says in Philippians that on that day every knee shall bow and every tongue shall confess that Jesus is Lord to the glory of God the Father (2:10-11). This is the focus of our Christian hope.

Alexander Maclaren, a great preacher of the last century, wrote on one occasion (and I have repeated these words at many a graveside over the years):

The primitive church thought more about the second coming than about death or heaven. They were not looking for a cleft in the ground called a grave; they were looking for a cleavage in the sky called Glory. They were not waiting for the undertaker; they were waiting for the Uppertaker. 'For the Lord himself shall descend from heaven, with a shout, with the archangel's call and the trumpet of God. We shall be caught up together to meet the Lord in the air, and so shall we ever be with the Lord.'

5

ITS CHALLENGE

The return of Christ challenges believers to work
The return of Christ challenges us
to make ourselves clean
The return of Christ challenges us to watch
The return of Jesus Christ challenges us to worship
The return of Jesus Christ challenges us to wait

5

Bible prophecy over the years has attracted its fair measure of cranks. Christianity, like most other movements, has its lunatic fringe; and the lunatic fringe have very often fastened on to prophecy as being one way of expressing their lunacy.

For example, one such expression occurred in the nineteenth century, led by a man called William Miller. Miller became notorious for setting dates for the coming again of Jesus. He announced first that Christ would return between March 21, 1842 and March 21, 1843. During that year, the Millerites were to get ready. Christ didn't return then, so Miller revised his estimate and said that Christ would definitely return between October 20 and October 24, 1844. He didn't.

Five years later, William Miller died and on his gravestone was put a statement which probably was the best piece of theology ever ascribed to the Millerite movement: 'At the appointed time, the end shall come.'

Now just in case you think that that is all in the past, let me refer to something that I read in an issue of *The Independent* in 1990. Six American Army Intelligence codebreakers who went missing from their unit in West Germany were arrested in Florida. All six are Christian fundamentalists who believe in the Rapture, a phenomenon related to the second coming of Jesus, whereby the faithful are supposed to be swept into heaven seven years before the return of Christ to the world. The Rapture was due to take place on Florida's Pensacola Beach that October.

I don't know what it is about prophecy that seems to get people's attention. My theory is that it has to do with knowing something which no one else knows; being in the know when everyone else is in the dark.

If Christians have learned anything about the second coming, they have learned first of all that it is *sure*. Jesus is coming again, and that certainty is built upon God's promise as well as upon God's activity in the resurrection of Jesus himself. But we have seen that Jesus' coming will be *sudden*. At a time when you do not expect him, the Son of Man will come. When everybody is saying, 'Peace, peace,' and 'Security, security,' the Bible says that suddenly the Son of Man will appear in space and time, in history. This means, therefore, that we cannot be sure whether Jesus may come within the next year, or within the next fifty years.

So what are we to do in the meantime? That is the challenge of his coming.

Interestingly, the passages of the Bible which refer to the second coming of Jesus emphasise how believers are to behave until then. They make clear that the meantime is not a time for speculation, but a time for action. Almost without exception every reference in the New Testament to the coming again of Jesus Christ is followed by an exhortation to holiness, to patience, or to service.

The great contrast between the Christian's interest in the future, and the interest that people take in astrology or in the New Age movement is this: while most people are interested to satisfy their curiosity, biblical prophecy is given to make people holy. It is in the light of that emphasis that I will suggest five aspects concerning the challenge of his coming.

1. The return of Christ challenges believers to work

There is a notion that believing in the second coming of Jesus somehow or other leads to opting out of responsibilities. The Bible addresses this notion head-on.

Take for example, the parable of the ten minas that Jesus tells in Luke 19:11-27. (A mina was a unit of money—about 100 days wages.) The parable tells how a king gave these coins to ten of his servants and told them to put the money to work until he came back. When he returned he challenged the three he had left with the money to come and show him what they had done with it.

Two of them had used the money wisely, so his investment had grown. But the third had buried the money and did not use it. The first two received the king's reward; the third was left to endure the king's judgment.

The message of the parable is simply this: in light of our Master's return we are to live responsibly, we are to work diligently, we are to plan wisely, we are to think realistically. We are to invest our time, our talents, our money carefully, in the interests of the kingdom.

Or take the parable of the returning master in Matthew 24:45. Jesus there implies that when the master comes back, he expects his servants to be busy at his work. Not engrossed in their own interests, not doing their own thing, not pleasing themselves, but doing his work, involved in his business. The parallel Jesus draws for us is simply this: that every Christian is a servant of one Master, Jesus Christ.

Each one has been given a work which only they can do. All have spiritual gifts which are unique in their combination to them as individuals. All have natural talents which are distinct to them as individuals. All have circumstances in their lives that are peculiar to them as individuals. All have contacts with other people that are special to them as individuals.

The challenge of the Bible is that when the Master comes back, he wants to find his people working, doing the things that are to hand, the things that he has left them to do. What are these things?

I will mention three that are found in Scripture. First of all, the Master wants to find us doing our duty when he comes. What is our duty? Surely our duty is simply the daily round, the common task. What we do in our home — rearing the children; doing an honest day's work for our employer; the project that we are working on for college or university or school. Doing our duty is doing the things that are to hand that need to be done.

Secondly, the Master wants to find us spreading the gospel when he comes. Not sitting on the gospel, not keeping a lid on the good news of Jesus Christ. Christians are to take the good news out to the world in its need. As Jesus said in Matthew 24:14: 'The gospel of the kingdom is to be preached throughout all the nations and then the end will come'.

What are we doing when we are evangelising, when we are reaching out to men and women across the world with the Good News of Jesus? We are hastening the day, says the apostle Peter, when the Lord Jesus will come back again. Spreading the gospel is helping bring back the King into this world.

Thirdly, Jesus, when he returns, wants to find us loving our neighbour. The great passage in Matthew that records the judgment of the Last Day reveals the primary concern of Jesus as he judges and evaluates the lives of men and women on his return:

[Jesus said,] 'When the Son of Man comes in his glory, and all the angels with him, he will sit on his throne in heavenly glory. All the nations will be gathered before him, and he will separate the people one from another as a shepherd separates the sheep from the goats. He will put the sheep on his right and the goats on his left.

'Then the King will say to those on his right, "Come, you who are blessed by my Father; take your inheritance, the kingdom prepared for you since the creation of the world. For I was hungry and you gave me something to eat, I was thirsty and you gave me something to drink, I was a stranger and you invited me in, I needed clothes and you clothed me, I was sick and you looked after me, I was in prison and you came to visit me."

'Then the righteous will answer him, "Lord, when did we see you hungry and feed you, or thirsty and give you something to drink? When did we see you a stranger and invite you in, or needing clothes and clothe you? When did we see you sick or in prison and go to visit you?"

'The King will reply, "I tell you the truth, whatever you did for one of the least of these brothers of mine, you did for me."

'Then he will say to those on his left, "Depart from me, you who are cursed, into the eternal fire prepared for the devil and his angels. For I was hungry and you gave me nothing to eat, I was thirsty and you gave me nothing to drink, I was a stranger and you did not invite me in, I needed clothes and you did not clothe me, I was sick and in prison and you did not look after me."

'They also will answer, "Lord, when did we see you hungry or thirsty or a stranger or needing clothes or sick or in prison, and did not help you?"

'He will reply, "I tell you the truth, whatever you did not do for one of the least of these, you did not do for me."

'Then they will go away to eternal punishment, but the righteous to eternal life.' (Matthew 25:31-46)

What have you been doing to the people who needed you in the world? What have you done for the poor, the prisoners? What have you done with those who were in need at your door? Did you respond to their need? Or did you ignore their need? Jesus wants to find us feeding the hungry, caring for the sick, visiting the prisoner, responding to the needy.

It is in light of the Lord's return that Paul says, 'Never tire of doing what is right' (2 Thessalonians 3:13). I read somewhere that there are still some Christians who think that manual labour is the president of Mexico! The Master when he comes wants to find us getting involved with the needs which are at hand. He wants to find us working.

So the challenge of Christ's return is to work hard, to reorder your private world, to get your act together, to be up and doing. Now when you have worked out 'manual labour', let's move on to the second point.

2. The return of Christ challenges us to make ourselves clean

In the New Testament, 'purify' is very often translated from a word which means simply 'to wash'. It has to do with holiness, which relates to the purging out of all that is unclean and unworthy in our lives, all the moral filth that is there. Look at these passages:

In 1 John 3:2,3 we read this:

'Dear friends, now we are children of God, and what we will be has not yet been made known. But we know that when he appears, we shall be like him, for we shall see him as he is. Everyone

who has this hope in him *purifies* himself, just
as he is pure'.

Paul wrote to Titus:

'For the grace of God that brings salvation has
appeared to all men [a reference to Christ's first
coming]. It teaches us to say "No" to ungodli-
ness and worldly passions, and to live self-
controlled, upright and godly lives in this present
age, while we wait for the blessed hope — the
glorious appearing of our great God and Saviour, Jesus Christ, who gave himself for us to
redeem us from all wickedness and to purify for
himself a people that are his very own, eager to
do what is good' (Titus 2:11-14).

What both John and Paul are saying is this: that
when our minds are on the coming of Jesus, we
begin to live consciously in the light of that coming. It begins to dominate our thinking and our
feeling and our decision-making, so that every
other influence is overwhelmed by that influence
of the coming again of the Master.

Take the image that is used in Ephesians 4 of
Christ as the bridegroom, and his people, the
church, as his bride. The great concern of Paul is
that the bride should be purified and washed and
cleansed and prepared for the bridegroom when he
comes.

Sometimes a girl's fiancé can be away on a journey or perhaps on business. When he comes back it will be their wedding day. This focuses her mind. Every other rival has no place within the orbit of her vision. Her mind is focused on that individual and on that event. Paul says there is a marriage we were made for as the people of God. We are to be married to Jesus, our heavenly bridegroom. Our wedding ought to have an effect on the way we live now, with our eyes focused on him, purifying ourselves even as he is pure.

How can we make such a commitment to purity? We must learn to live by short accounts. We must refuse to allow the filth in our lives to stack up. We must refuse to allow ourselves to ignore even the little things that have broken our fellowship with God or with others. We are to come to Jesus and let Jesus wash us regularly. John says this in 1 John 1:9: 'If we confess our sins, he is faithful and just and will forgive us our sins and purify us from all unrighteousness.'

Are we keeping short accounts in our relationship with God? Are we confessing our sins daily to him? Are we allowing the Lord to wash us clean from our sins? When he comes back will he find us washed, ready to go?

3. The return of Christ challenges us to watch

No-one knows about that day or hour, not even the angels in heaven, nor the Son, but only the Father. Be on guard! Be alert! You do not know when that time will come. It's like a man going away: He leaves his house and puts his servants in charge, each with his assigned task, and tells the one at the door to keep watch. Therefore keep watch because you do not know when the owner of the house will come back — whether in the evening, or at midnight, or when the cock crows, or at dawn. If he comes suddenly, do not let him find you sleeping. What I say to you, I say to everyone: 'Watch!' (Mark 13:32-37).

To watch is the great theme of those verses in Mark 13. Did you notice how that idea recurred again and again? Be on guard, be alert, watch. Why? For no one knows about that day or hour, not even the angels of heaven, not even the Son, far less William Miller or whoever it was that was going to be at Pensacola Beach, Florida, in October 1990! Only the Father knows, so be on guard! Be alert!

In light of the urgency of the coming again of Jesus, isn't it amazing that so few of us have, in the daily routine of our lives, even one fleeting conscious thought that Jesus may return today? How many of us make decisions and plans, draw up schemes and yet never once allow it to enter into our heads that Jesus may interrupt those plans and those schemes.

C. S. Lewis said that because church members are so comfortable in this world they cannot bring themselves to think about going to another. Is that true of us? And yet the reason why the Bible speaks of the certainty of Christ's return and also of the uncertainty of its timing, is that we will be continually watching, continually on our guard, continually in a state of readiness.

One of the themes that is very often related to this theme of watching, is the theme of *prayer*: Watch and pray. It seems right that we should not only look for Jesus' appearing, but that we should be praying for his appearing.

Do you remember what Jesus taught us to pray in that model prayer? *Your kingdom come*. When we pray this request, we are praying that the kingdom of God which is invisible and hidden and in our hearts, would be made visible, and open, and public for the universe to see. We are praying that Jesus would come back in a great revelation of his glory. We are praying for the end of history.

The early Christians used the Aramaic word *Maranatha* – Our Lord come – as a prayer. Paul so uses it in 1 Corinthians 16:22. In Revelation 22:17, the Holy Spirit is seen to be pleading in unison with the church of Jesus Christ for the return of the Lord: 'The Spirit and the bride say, Come!' The apostle John almost closes the entire Bible as well as his book with the prayer, 'Come, Lord Jesus.'

Are we living, looking and longing for his appearing? Are we watching for the appearing of our great God and Saviour Jesus Christ? Maybe we need to get into the habit as we wake up each morning of saying to the Lord, 'Good morning, Lord, will I see you today?'

We are to watch.

4. The return of Jesus Christ challenges us to worship

Worship lies at the heart of the Christian life. Mankind was created to worship. The Shorter Catechism reminds us that 'the chief end of man is to glorify God and enjoy him for ever'. Worship is the highest activity of which redeemed men and women are capable. In the book of Revelation we are told that the great occupation of saints in the presence of God will be to worship 'him who sits on the throne ... and the Lamb'. In Revelation 5:9, we find this expressed in the redeemed gathering singing the 'new song', the song of Moses and the Lamb, the song of praise and adoration to our King Jesus.

One of the ways worship is expressed is in praise. Praise focuses on the mighty acts of God in Christ. It celebrates the saving career of Jesus in his birth, life, death and resurrection. It expresses thankfulness for God's work in our life, in choosing us, in calling us, in saving us and in keeping us. But it also looks forward to the return of Christ, the glory of the new heaven and earth, the fulness of the kingdom that is coming. Worship involves the glad anticipation of that day when God's love and holiness will be vindicated before a watching world.

So, in some of the early hymns which have found their way into the New Testament, we find this focus represented. In the famous 'Christ Hymn' in Philippians 2 the climax affirms that

... at the name of Jesus every knee should bow ...
and every tongue confess that Jesus Christ is Lord,
to the glory of God the Father (verse 10-11).

Central to Christian worship is the Lord's Supper which John Calvin called 'a visible word of God'. The Lord's Supper looks back to our Lord's agonies and death and the salvation he achieved for us. How long are we to gather round the Lord's table? How long are we to hold in our hands the elements that represent our Saviour's body and blood? Paul tells us we are 'to do this ... until he comes' (1 Corinthians 11:26).

The second coming of Jesus Christ is a great stimulus to worship because it will be the realisation of the triumph of God, the final overthrow of suffering, death, sin and the powers of darkness. It will be the final, public and universal revelation and acknowledgement that Jesus is Lord, to the glory of God the Father.

5. The return of Jesus Christ challenges us to wait

Over and over again, you will find the word *wait* used of the coming again of Jesus. Very often it is in connection with the word *patience*. That is the way it is used in James 5:7-8: Consider, be patient, until the Lord comes. James uses the picture of a farmer who sows the seed and then waits with patience until the harvest time arrives. There is nothing he can do to hurry the harvest, nothing he can do to precipitate the events of the harvest. He has to wait with patience. The winds may blow and the rains may come, there may be lightning storms and there may be hurricanes, there may be all kinds of things but having planted the seed, all he can do is wait.

The writer of the book of Hebrews speaks about the Christian hope as an anchor for the soul — we have cast our anchor in God. But we do not all of a sudden receive everything that God has promised to those who love him. We do not suddenly have the perfect health, the perfect healing and the perfect wholeness that God promises to his people. Generally in this life, although we cast our anchor in God the moment we are converted, temptations increase rather than diminish. The circumstances of life get harder instead of easier, and the way to heaven seems to become more difficult instead of less difficult. The word of Scripture is: Wait with patience. Don't allow anything to rob you of waiting for the appearing of our glorious God and Saviour Jesus Christ.

The world will ask scoffingly: 'Where is the promise of his coming? Why is he taking his time?' Tell them that God is showing patience with them, for he is not willing that any should perish but all should come to repentance. Be patient, wait with patience (2 Peter 3:4,8).

But this word *wait*, in the New Testament, is often linked to the word *hope*. The world has many wishes about the future.

When communism collapsed in Eastern Europe and the Soviet Union, some people spoke of 'a new world order'. Politicians talked about the 'peace dividend' as the need for military spending was reduced. But the 'peace' achieved increasingly looks like an illusion with the rise of nationalism and the outbreak of civil violence. The future is less than certain.

The world has great hopes for the future. Somehow or other it hopes to control its environmental damage, its pollution and the hole in the ozone layer and be able to reduce the number of nuclear weapons and other i...

The world has grea...
are only wishes. The Ch...
hope because it is a certain...
sure and certain as an anch...
[Christ] will appear a secon...
salvation to those who are wait...
brews 9:28).

Or take these words in Romans ...5, where
Paul says: 'We wait eagerly for our adoption as
sons.' In fact he proceeds to make a great argument
as to why we have not yet received all that God has
promised to us — because if we did have it, what
would we be waiting for? But he says we are saved
in hope, therefore we wait for it, patiently.

In 1 Thessalonians 1:9-10 we have a statement
of genuine Christian experience, a report Paul had
heard about the Thessalonian believers: 'They tell
how you turned to God from idols to serve the
living and true God, and to wait for his Son from
heaven, whom he raised from the dead — Jesus,
who rescues us from the coming wrath'. Notice
three words that Paul uses here — turning, serving,
waiting. They seem to me to be about the best
summary you can find about the Christian life.

It begins when you turn — that's conversion.
To be converted means to turn right round, from
going your way to start going God's way. It's a
change of mind leading to a change of direction.

...s turned to God from idols, they ...ng behind, but now they have turned ...s God, he is the direction they are going in ...ow. That is repentance and faith. That is conversion. That is how you become a Christian. So what do you do now? You serve the living and true God. That is how you occupy your time. The question is, when Jesus comes will we be found ready?

I came across this story of an incident, a number of years ago, when the former President Eisenhower of the USA was taking his summer vacation in Denver, Colorado. His attention was drawn to a letter in a local newspaper which told how a six year-old boy, Paul Haley, was dying of incurable cancer. He had expressed a wish to see the President of the United States. In one of those spontaneous gestures for which Eisenhower came to be remembered, he decided to go and see the boy.

The big presidential limousine pulled up one August Sunday morning in front of the house. Everything was quiet in the neighbourhood. Out of the limousine got the President, who went up and knocked at the door. It was opened by Mr. Donald Haley with his son, Paul, just behind him. Don Haley was wearing blue jeans and an old shirt with a day's growth of beard. He had just wakened up and he wasn't in the best of form. There, to his amazement, standing at his front door, was the President of the United States.

You can imagine how in the little town for years afterwards, the conversation was of the day the President came to visit the Haley household. People were thrilled. All that is, except Mr. Haley, who could never forget how he was dressed when he opened the door. Those jeans, that old shirt, that unshaven face. What a way to meet the President of the United States!

We are expecting the arrival of the King of kings and Lord of lords. We are expecting his arrival, the appearance at our door of the ruler of the universe. We are expecting and we are looking for him. But are we ready?

Are we working, doing the job God has put at our hand?

Are we washing, keeping clean; that is, keeping short accounts with God to ensure we remain pure, up-to-date in our cleansing from sin?

Are we watching? Not in the unbalanced way that the Millerites did, but in a balanced, sensible disposition, watching and praying for the coming again of Jesus?

Are we worshipping? Are we learning how to engage our emotions, as well as our minds and our lips, in this business of articulating the praises of our King Jesus, so it won't be a big shock for us when he comes back?

Are we waiting? Are we waiting in patience? And in hope? With a confidence growing within us as the days pass, that when he comes we shall rise to meet him with joy?

The Lord Jesus challenges us to work; he challenges us to cleanse our hearts and our lives; he challenges us to watch, to be ready, to be on the look-out, to be praying for his coming; he challenges us to worship; and he challenges us to wait.

6

ITS IMMINENCE

Signs which evidence the grace of God
Signs which indicate opposition to God
Signs indicating the judgment of God

6

We have already looked at the certainty, the manner, the purpose and the challenge of the second coming. In this chapter we will consider its imminence and in particular the signs of the times.

What do we mean when we say the Lord is at hand or the coming of the Lord Jesus is near? Particularly, what do we mean in the light of the fact that the Bible often speaks of the signs of the times? What I would like you to do is put aside any preconceived ideas of what the signs of the times are, and what they relate to, and we will try and discover what the Bible means by that expression.

Matthew 16:1-4 are key verses that we need to look at in order to understand what is meant by this expression, the signs of the times. In this passage the Pharisees and the Sadducees come to Jesus, pestering him, asking him to show them a sign from heaven. He replied (verses 2-3): 'When evening comes, you say, "It will be fair weather, for the sky is red," and in the morning, "Today it

will be stormy, for the sky is red and overcast."
You know how to interpret the appearance of the
sky, but you cannot interpret the signs of the
times.'

The word 'sign' in the New Testament means a
meaningful, God-given token, indicating what
God has done or what he is doing or what he is
about to do. The word, 'times', as it is used here,
is the Greek word *cheiros*, which in the New
Testament refers to a period of God's activity in
which people may come to faith in Jesus Christ. A
classic verse illustrating the use of the word is in 2
Corinthians where Paul says: 'Now is the time of
God's favour; now is the day of salvation' (6:2).

So the 'signs of the times' refers to a period of
time in which God is working, in which men and
women may come to faith in Christ; a period of
time in which there are signs or tokens that tell us
the period is here, has arrived.

Before we look at the signs in particular, we
have to understand that this expression, the signs of
the times, refers first of all to what God has done.
That is very obvious from Matthew 16:3. Jesus is
here criticising the religious leaders of his day for
not recognising the signs of the Messiah's presence with them. He is saying to these religious
leaders: 'You cannot see the signs of the times?
They are here, they have arrived, they are present.
They are being demonstrated all around just now.

They are obvious for you, and yet you cannot see that the Messiah has come, that he has arrived.'

Jesus earlier had sent a message to John the Baptist who was doubting whether he was reading the signs of the times correctly. Look at the message Jesus sent: 'The blind receive sight, the lame walk, those who have leprosy are cured, the deaf hear, the dead are raised, and the good news is preached to the poor' (Matthew 11:5). These, Jesus is saying to these religious leaders, are the signs of the time. God has intervened in history; God has come to initiate the period of grace, the time for men to repent and believe the gospel.

In Matthew 16:4, Jesus proceeds to tell them that the particular sign he will give them is the sign of Jonah, who was three days in the belly of the fish and then was brought back to land. Jesus is obviously referring to his own three-day stay in the tomb, which was followed by his resurrection from the dead.

The signs of the times, then, first of all indicate what God has done. They tell us God has intervened in history, in Christ, and that a decisive change has occurred in the history of the human race. Christ has initiated an era of grace in which men and women may come to faith in him.

Secondly, the signs indicate not only what God has done, but they also point to what he is doing. Jesus, in the parable of the wheat and the tares

(Matthew 13:24-30), teaches that the wheat and the weeds grow together, alongside one another, until the harvest at the end of the age. The point of the parable is that the war between the forces of God on the one hand, and the forces of Satan and evil on the other, is to continue throughout the whole course of this age.

The signs of the times bear witness to this ongoing struggle. Some of the signs, such as the preaching of the gospel, remind us that this is the age in which the power of God is at work for the salvation of men and women who will believe in Jesus. Other signs, like the growth of apostasy and lawlessness, show that Antichrist and antichristian forces are presently operating in the world, in conflict with the powers of God. This calls for continual watchfulness on the part of Christians.

Thirdly, the signs point forward to the climactic moment when Jesus Christ will return in power and in glory. It may very well be that the signs given in the Bible are to intensify towards the end of the age. Nevertheless, the signs of the times which are ever present tell us that God has come in Christ, that the kingdoms of this world and the Kingdom of God are at loggerheads, and that Jesus is coming to bring an end to history.

So it is quite wrong, then, to think of the signs of the times as primarily referring to events that will happen just immediately prior to the end of history. They are there continually, and we are always right to look for them and to see them.

Now let us look at the signs of the times. We are going to classify them under three headings.

1. Signs which evidence the grace of God

I have already explained how this time is the time of salvation when God is extending to the world the opportunity for men and women to come to faith in Jesus. The *cheiros* of opportunity extends from the first coming of Jesus to the second coming of Jesus. Those two comings bracket, if you will, this period of activity in which God is offering salvation to the world.

There are two signs of this type that we need to notice during this period.

The Gospel
First, there is the proclamation of the gospel to all the nations.

When we read the Old Testament prophets, we discover that they speak of the last days as being ushered in by the Holy Spirit, who would be poured out upon all flesh. That is an Old Testament expression indicating that when the Holy Spirit comes in the last days, he will come not only to Jews but also to Gentiles. All flesh will experience the work of the Holy Spirit in the last days. Isaiah says in chapter 52 that the ends of the earth would see the salvation of the Lord. Messiah would be a light for the nations. All flesh would see the glory of the Lord.

When we come to the New Testament, we find the Lord Jesus making this specific promise in Matthew 24:14: 'This gospel of the kingdom will be preached in the whole world as a testimony to all nations [that is Gentile nations], and then the end will come.'

Now we need to be clear about what Jesus is saying in verse 14. He is not saying that all the nations will be converted or everybody in the world will be converted. Nor is he even saying that all individuals necessarily must hear the gospel themselves. But what he is saying is that during this period between his departure and his reappearance, the gospel of the kingdom will become a force to be reckoned with, not only within Judaism, but in the world at large. The world will have to come to terms with his claims, with his gospel, with his commands and with his message.

He is saying that one of the signs of the times is the missionary expansion of the Church. You remember this is what he said to his disciples when he was departing from them just before his ascension into heaven: 'But you will receive power when the Holy Spirit comes on you; and you will be my witnesses in Jerusalem, and in all Judaea and Samaria, and to the ends of the earth' (Acts 1:8).

The hallmark of this time, this age of grace in which we live, is the missionary expansion of the Church.

Here is a sign then that points back to the arrival of Jesus and the gospel events. It points to the present, to the preaching of the gospel that is going on just now; it points to the future, for then the end will come, after this word of the gospel has been preached as a testimony to all the nations. This places upon every generation the task of bringing the gospel to every nation. For only God will know when this sign has been completely fulfilled, the preaching of the gospel to all peoples.

The Jews
The second sign which reveals the grace of God is the salvation of the fullness of Israel. Paul discusses this in Romans 11:25-27:

> I do not want you to be ignorant of this mystery, brothers, so that you may not be conceited: Israel has experienced a hardening in part until the full number of the Gentiles has come in. And so all Israel will be saved, as it is written:
>
> > 'The deliverer will come from Zion:
> > > he will turn godlessness away from Jacob.
> > And this is my covenant with them
> > > when I take away their sins.'

In those verses Paul both speaks about Israel, the nation, and about Israel, the people of God. Israel, the people of God, is now no longer simply a racial grouping, but it is an international fellowship of everybody who has come to trust in Jesus Christ.

Today, Israel the nation has been set aside. But some of those who belong to Israel, the nation, have become part of Israel, the people of God, because they have come to faith in the Lord Jesus. Throughout this age, there will be Jews who will come to faith in Jesus, who will see through the hardness and the blindness of their unbelief to Jesus, the Messiah who has come, and they will become part of the people of God.

Paul may also be saying here that the number of Jews turning to Jesus may increase towards the end of history. There will be a time prior to the coming again of the Lord Jesus Christ when the numbers of converted Jews will increase. Under this heading I believe we would have to say that the establishment of the state of Israel in 1948 had no direct bearing on the fulfilment of this particular promise. At least not then. More Jews live outside of Israel than live in Israel.

Although the creation of the state of Israel has focused the minds and the eyes of the world upon the Jews as a race, the increasing number of Jews that are being reported coming to faith in Christ in

North America, in South America and in the Far East, has yet to be matched by a similar turning to Christ of Jews now resident in Israel. We need to be praying for and working for the conversion of Israeli Jews to the Lord Jesus Christ.

The signs tell us then, that right now in this age, Jews will be converted, that their conversion is a sign of Christ's return, and that we need to continue to share the gospel with them. They are signs which indicate the grace of God and they are occurring just now.

2. Signs which indicate opposition to God
Three features are mentioned in the Bible as signs of the times indicating opposition to God.

Tribulation
The word 'tribulation' means trouble. It is the word Jesus uses in John 16:33 when he says to his disciples: 'In this world you will have trouble'. Tribulation is to be characteristic of the child of God throughout the age. In Revelation 7 reference is made to the Great Tribulation. I think we should understand that word *great* not so much as a period of intense tribulation at the end of history, but as a word which denotes the length of the trouble. It is the Great Tribulation for the simple reason that it goes on for so long, from the departure of Jesus until his reappearance in history.

In Matthew 24, the disciples asked Jesus two distinct questions, and that is why the passage is so often hard to understand. They had heard Jesus speaking about the temple in Jerusalem, and predicting that not one stone would be left on top of another. Because they linked the destruction of the temple with the end of the world, they came to Jesus and asked him, 'Tell us, when will this happen [when will the temple be destroyed], and what will be the sign of your coming and of the end of the age?' But they are two very distinct questions.

Jesus, in answering, describes and interweaves the answers to those two questions one with the other.

When he talks about those in Judaea fleeing to the mountains, he is referring to that period of time in Jewish history in AD 70, when the emperor Titus surrounded Jerusalem and besieged it. Many did indeed flee to the mountains and hid there to escape the wrath of the Roman soldiers. The Roman army entered Jerusalem and set up an image of the emperor (the Abomination of Desolation) in the temple. Then they destroyed it. The emperor decreed that not one stone should be left standing upon another. That was fulfilled. There was trouble then.

Jesus, however, says that there will be trouble throughout this age (verses 9-14). He links together the preaching of the gospel throughout the age and the trouble that will come throughout the same period. There will be persecution, and there will be betrayal. There will be false prophets, there will be coldness of heart and there will be departure from the faith.

Trouble is to be the hallmark of this age, intensifying apparently towards its end. But the tribulation which is present even today is a sign of the times in which we live, the time of opposition to God.

Apostasy

The word apostasy means to depart from the faith.

In the Old Testament, a whole generation of Israel, the people of God, turned away from him in the wilderness, and died there. During the time of the Judges, there were whole periods of Israel's history when they turned away from God. And in Matthew 24, Jesus says there will be those who will turn away from the faith (verse 10); and that the love of most will grow cold (verse 12). As we review the history of the church, we discover that every prediction of apostasy has been fulfilled over and over and over again.

Take the great churches to which the New Testament epistles were written — Corinth, Rome, Ephesus, Colosse, Sardis, Philadelphia, Smyrna, Thyatira, Laodicea, Pergamos. Most of them were in modern-day Turkey. Today, you would be hard-put to find five hundred believers there.

Look at Europe where occurred the great Reformation of the church, a great revival of spiritual life and understanding. It would be difficult to find living, vibrant evangelicalism in France, the home of Calvin, or Germany, the home of Luther.

Apostasy, as a mark of the church during this age, has been seen in revival and declension, spiritual renewal and spiritual death. Apostasy is a sign of the times covering the entire age.

Again it may very well be that this apostasy will intensify towards the end of the age. Paul does seem to suggest this in 2 Thessalonians 2:3 when he says: 'Don't let anyone deceive you in any way, for that day will not come until the rebellion occurs.'

In modern times, the intensification of apostasy in the western world began in the nineteenth century with higher criticism on the continent of Europe, which produced Modernism and Liberalism. This movement denied beliefs which had never been denied before in the history of the church — the bodily resurrection of Jesus, the virgin birth of Jesus, and other historic truths.

There certainly has been an intensification of apostasy in the last hundred years.

The Antichrist

The clearest teaching we have about Antichrist is in John's letters, towards the end of the New Testament.

He tells us that even then there were already many antichrists. Yes, he says, there is an Antichrist that is yet to come, but the sign of Antichrist is already apparent in the world (1 John 2:18). What is the sign of the Antichrist? The Antichrist is the one who denies the Father and the Son. He is the one who refuses to confess Jesus, who refuses to acknowledge the coming of Jesus Christ in the flesh.

Jesus speaks of antichrists in Matthew 24, when he says there are many false prophets, and false Christs that have gone into the world. Notice that — many of them. Jesus is saying that history is going to be littered with these false Christs and false prophets.

Titus, the Roman emperor who will besiege the holy city, would be an anticipation of the final Antichrist, and so would Napoleon, Hitler, and Mussolini. Believers have not been wrong to identify in their generation the forces of antichrist. For throughout this age, antichrist is an on-going sign to the people of God, a sign of the innate conflict and opposition to the things of God that has been aroused by the coming of Jesus Christ into history.

Jesus is the one who contradicts the ways of this

world. He has introduced an opposition unlike any other opposition that has ever been seen in history. Christianity provokes opposition from the world.

Paul teaches in 2 Thessalonians 2:1-10, that Antichrist, who is yet to come, will be a man of lawlessness:

> Concerning the coming of our Lord Jesus Christ and our being gathered to him, we ask you, brothers, not to become easily unsettled or alarmed by some prophecy, report or letter supposed to have come from us, saying that the day of the Lord has already come. Don't let anyone deceive you in any way, for that day will not come until the rebellion occurs and the man of lawlessness is revealed, the man doomed to destruction. He will oppose and will exalt himself over everything that is called God or is worshipped, so that he sets himself up in God's temple, proclaiming himself to be God.
>
> Don't you remember that when I was with you I used to tell you these things? And now you know what is holding him back, so that he may be revealed at the proper time. For the secret power of lawlessness is already at work; but the one who now holds it back will continue to do so till he is taken out of the way. And then the lawless one will be revealed, whom the Lord Jesus will overthrow with the breath of his mouth and destroy by the splendour of his

coming. The coming of the lawless one will be in accordance with the work of Satan displayed in all kinds of counterfeit miracles, signs and wonders, and in every sort of evil that deceives those who are perishing. They perish because they refused to love the truth and so be saved.

We need to be careful in our preconception of what Antichrist will be like. We must not think of Antichrist merely in dictatorial terms. The mark of Antichrist is not so much that he will necessarily impose his will on others. Rather, he will draw others to go his way, will make himself the one to be followed, the one whose policies are most attractive. He may be very nice and affable, but he will direct the attention of men and women away from Christ to put their confidence in himself.

He will be Antichrist (the word *anti*, in the Greek, means 'instead of' as well as 'opposed to'): he will make himself the world's redeemer and deliverer — economically, socially, racially, spiritually.

These three signs indicate the opposition to God.

3. Signs indicating the judgment of God

These are listed in Matthew 24:6-8: 'You will hear of wars and rumours of wars, but see to it that you are not alarmed. Such things must happen, but the end is still to come. Nation will rise against nation, and kingdom against kingdom. There will be famines and earthquakes in various places. All these are the beginning of birth pains.'

Now let me say some things about the signs which indicate divine judgment.

Firstly, these signs have their Old Testament antecedents. Wars, famines, earthquakes, are mentioned in the Old Testament as signs of God's judgment.

Secondly, these signs are the evidences of God's judgment in history. I do not mean that Jesus told his disciples that people who undergo suffering or death as a result of wars and disasters are any more the objects of God's wrath than anyone else. That is not the Bible's teaching. But it does mean that these signs are a manifestation of the fact that this present world ecologically, as well as individually, is under the curse of God.

Do you remember when man sinned in the Garden of Eden? God pronounced a curse not only on men and women but upon all of nature. It isn't only human society that is under the curse and the judgment of God, the whole created order is under the same curse and judgment. That is why there are weeds in your garden! And from that trivial matter right through the whole spectrum to earthquakes and hurricanes and famines, the world is under the curse of God.

These are the evidences in history of the judgment of God upon a fallen, sinful, corrupted, depraved race. We need to recognise that. Paul wrote in Romans 1:18: 'The wrath of God is being revealed from heaven' - not *will be*, pointing to the last judgment, but *is being* revealed from heaven now - 'against all the godlessness and wickedness of men'.

These natural disasters of wars and famines and earthquakes are signs, says Jesus, that the wrath of God is being revealed against the cursed world.

Why, for example, does war happen? War happens as the great token of man's sinfulness. Why does God permit it? Listen to these words preached in 1940 by Dr. Martin Lloyd-Jones: 'War is not to be viewed as the interruption of personal convenience and the enjoyments of life. Something far more serious is involved. War is divine judgment upon the very lives which men pursue. It is permitted in order that men may see through it more clearly than they have ever done before what sin really is and thus be led back to God.'

These disasters that we see are signs of the judgment of God. These awful expressions of man's inhumanity to man, from child abuse through to war, are all the evidences of the fact that we live in a fallen world, under the judgment of God that we bring upon ourselves. We need to say that to men and women today.

In the book of Revelation, there are several

overviews of human history and in them there is a description of these afflictions that we see all around us: diseases run wild, pollution run rampant, ecological disasters, famines, wars, and many more.

The first description we have of them is as seals, unlocked by the Lamb who is on the throne. These disasters do not happen by chance, they are part of God's overall control of history. Then they are seen from another angle: they are seen as trumpet blasts, calling men and women to repentance, to turn from their sin to the Lord whom they have left and disregarded. Finally, they are seen as bowls of wrath poured out on a sinful, unrepentant world because of its sin and its backsliding. The signs are evidences of God's judgment.

Thirdly, these signs are not strictly speaking signs of the end. You notice in Matthew 24:6 that the end is not yet, the end is still to come. 'All these are the beginning of the birth pains' (verse 8). They point towards the end, but they don't necessarily mean the end.

They point us to a better world. Do you notice how Jesus describes them there as 'birth pains'? Paul uses the very same root in Romans 8:22, when he says the whole creation is groaning as in the pains of childbirth until now. These movements and disasters, and other things that are happening in nature, are the groanings of creation as it looks forward to recreation in wholeness when the Lord Jesus comes back again.

Fourthly, these signs mark the entire period between Christ's first and second coming. They are signs to the believer that God is working his purpose out in history, that God takes sin seriously if we will not.

Fifthly, these signs are to be seen as God's trumpet-calls to a spiritually drowsy world. C. S. Lewis wrote: 'God whispers to us in our pleasures, God shouts to us in our pains.'

These signs of the times point us to the past. They tell us that God has intervened in human history. He has initiated something which is moving forwards towards the end of time. They point to that moment when Christ will come again in power and glory.

But they speak to us in the present. As Christian people they speak to us of our present duty to hasten the time of Christ's return by getting the gospel out to the world and by encouraging missionary work among Jews.

They speak to us about opposition, the sign of contradiction that the Cross is to men and women who are without Jesus. Because we are in a conflict, we can expect to suffer trouble of one kind or another. We should not be caught off guard when we see church leaders denying the very foundations of the faith. We ought not to be surprised when we see leaders who lead people not in the ways of righteousness, but in the ways of lawlessness.

We ought not to be caught off guard by the natural disasters, the wars, the trials and the strife that we see in the world, for we live in a moral universe that is moving forward inexorably towards the day when God will judge the world in righteousness by the man he has appointed, Jesus Christ the Righteous One.

7

ITS REALITY

The return of Jesus Christ will be
the ultimate event
The return of Jesus will mark
the ultimate experience
The return of Jesus will produce
the ultimate environment
The return of Christ will produce
the ultimate enjoyment
The return of Christ will enlist us in
the ultimate employment

7

As we have seen in the previous chapters the second coming of Christ has come before us in various ways. It is the goal of the Christian life; it is the focus of the Christian hope; it is the terminus of human history. It is therefore the end and the beginning of life. It is the end of life as we know it, and it is the beginning of life as we have not yet discovered it.

But what will it be like when Jesus comes again? It is one thing to look at the Bible and see the facts of his coming, to understand the order in which events will take place and to know something of the signs of the times that prepare us for the arrival of our King. But what will it be like for you and me when Jesus Christ appears?

On this subject, we are like sightseers looking at some spectacle out on the horizon, away in the distance. We can make out, as it were, an outline, but we are left guessing at the reality that it represents just out of our sight. You will be disappointed if you look in the Bible for details of that day and its aftermath. There is a gigantic gulf that exists between life now as we are experiencing it, and life then when Jesus comes again. There is a sense in which what we are going to do in this chapter is to push out towards the outer limits of our Christian knowledge, towards the boundaries of any understanding which the Bible has given us of what it will be like when Jesus comes again. But we have to do it.

We have to do it because the return of Jesus is the final stage in the drama of God's activity which began with creation; followed by the Incarnation when God became a human being, then the work of Christ on the cross, his Resurrection and the outpouring of the Spirit; and finishes with the return of Jesus Christ at the end of history. These are the great movements of God's activity towards us. We were converted with a view to this great event for it is the final stage of the salvation process.

When you became a Christian you may have wondered to yourself - Is this it? Is this why I gave my life to Christ? Is this why I make the daily sacrifice that is involved in obedience? Is this all that is in store for me as a Christian? I am afraid that many Christians think that it is. So they run here and there and try this and that, looking for some kind of supernatural input into their lives that will

make their present commitment to Jesus worth-
while. Therefore, we must look at the second
coming, for it proclaims to us that the present is not
all God has for us.

What will it mean when Christ returns?

1. The return of Jesus Christ will be the ultimate event

History has known great and splendid occasions.
Modern means of communication have brought
many great events into our living rooms, beginning I am told, at the very boundary of my own
memory, I have to say, with the coronation of
Queen Elizabeth II, which was shown on televi-
sions, to those who owned them in those days, and
in halls up and down the country. Beginning with
an event which was so spectacular in its day, to
later events like the American bicentenary in 1976,
or the French bicentenary of the Revolution, more
recently. These splendid events captured the imagination and the attention of the world.

But all of those events will pale into insignificance in comparison with this event of Jesus Christ
coming in spectacular splendour to reign. Paul
says, in 2 Thessalonians 1:7-10: 'This will happen
when the Lord Jesus is revealed from heaven in
blazing fire, with his powerful angels ... on the day
he comes to be glorified in his holy people and to
be marvelled at among all those who have be-

lieved'. It is going to be a spectacular occasion; it is going to be the ultimate event.

You and I are not going to be mere spectators of that event. Unlike the coronation we will not be sitting far from it watching it on TV, or in a cinema hall watching it on a large screen. Nor will we even be like those in the crowd watching the procession of the royals going by. The Bible tells us that you and I who are believers are going to be participants in that event: 'caught up,' says Paul to the Thessalonians, 'to be with the Lord in the air'. And then coming with the Lord, descending as part of his royal retinue to planet Earth, to accomplish his great purposes. Never in our wildest dreams have we ever come close to imagining the thrill and ecstasy of that occasion. When Christ who is our life appears, then we also will appear with him in glory. What an event! A spectacular event.

Not only that. It is going to be an event at which we will meet the Lord Jesus. Have you ever imagined some great occasion where you might be introduced to some famous personality? I remember the day when Princess Diana came to town, and I was standing outside a shop. I just happened to be there at that time, and she waved to me - there was nobody else for her to wave to! She waved to me at that point! I walked along the main street to see whether I could get into the crowd and be there when she did her little walk around and maybe she would shake my hand. Ever thought what a tremendous thing it would be to shake the hand of somebody really famous? And yet, all of those fantastic opportunities pale into insignificance. The Lord himself will descend from heaven, with a cry of command, and we will be caught up to meet him in the air. We will meet the Lord Jesus. The return of Jesus will be the ultimate event.

2. The return of Jesus will mark the ultimate experience

The experience I am referring to is Christian experience which, at present, is partial and varied.

Take the experience of conversion. All Christian believers are converted, but we are all converted at different times, through different means, and in different circumstances. Some can remember the moment of their conversion; others cannot.

Similarly, we are given the Holy Spirit. For some the awareness of the Spirit is powerful and strong. They have great experiences when their hearts are ravished by his presence, and by the love of Jesus that the Holy Spirit inevitably and invariably engenders within us. But even at its best, even at its highest, our experience of the Holy Spirit is only the foretaste of something that is yet to come.

Take our experience of spiritual gifting. Some are, it seems, blessed amazingly with graces and gifts. We look at their lives and we see them manifesting so clearly the likeness of Jesus, being so useful in God's service, and we feel ourselves to be so inadequate and so lacking in gifts.

We don't always feel that we are experiencing joy unspeakable and full of glory. We came to Christ believing that he would make all things new within us, but we see in ourselves old habits, old scars, old attitudes. Perhaps we came to Christ believing the implication sometimes made in Christian preaching, that all our problems would be solved there and then. But ill health continues to dog us; temptation continues to frustrate us; death continues to frighten us.

We need to remember what Paul wrote in Romans 8, that we are saved 'in hope'. *Salvation* is a word with a future tense. We shall be saved. We invite people to come to Christ *now*, in order that they might experience something *then*. The Bible teaches concerning this final experience of full salvation that you and I shall all receive it at one and the same time. Nobody will have this experience before another. It does not matter how mature one person is spiritually, no matter how much he has been used by God; all believers will experience full salvation at the same time. We shall be caught up together to be with the Lord, and our experience of full salvation will be given to us then.

And that experience will be a total experience. It won't be simply a spiritual experience. We have spiritual experiences of God now; we have experienced times of joy when we are praising and worshipping God. By and large, our experiences now are spiritual, they are internal, they can't be seen. But it won't be a spiritual experience alone.

Incidentally, this is so superior to that offered by the New Age movement, borrowing as it does from Buddhism. The New Age movement offers to people this destiny: eventually, it says, the real person, the consciousness, is going to lose consciousness of itself, and is going to be caught up eventually as reincarnation takes place, and as history moves forward, into a sort of universal consciousness, where we lose sight of ourselves and become part of the universal mind. I don't know about you, but that doesn't turn me on very much. It doesn't really grip my imagination. I don't really want to lose my mind or lose my sense of identity, or lose my consciousness of being me. That's no hope at all.

The Christian hope is that we will have a total experience that will touch both body and spirit. What will it be like when Jesus comes? What will our experience be then?

Well, get this: instantaneously we will have *perfect knowledge*, not exhaustive knowledge, mark you, for we won't become omniscient like God. But there will be accurate knowledge. We have questions now that we would like answered. There are gaps in our understanding. Some things that are happening to us or are happening in the world or have happened in the past don't make sense to us. Sometimes life is like a detective plot with one vital clue missing. But the Bible says, 'But now we see a poor reflection as in a mirror; then we shall see face to face. Now I know in part; then I shall know fully, even as I am fully known.'

Have you ever asked the question, Why? Why did this happen to that person? On the day when we see Jesus, all of the bits will fit into place, and we will have perfect knowledge, for the answers will be ours.

Further we will have *perfect holiness*. At present we are unholy, for we constantly sin and we must constantly be asking God for forgiveness. But the Bible says in 1 John 3:2: *We know that when he appears, we shall be like him*. We shall be like Jesus in mind and body. We shall be like him in thought and action. We shall be perfectly like him.

What does that mean? Well, it means that when Jesus returns and I am caught up to be with him, all of a sudden I will be delivered, at that moment, from the pull of my sinful nature. Do you live with that pull? Do you know what Paul is referring to in Romans 7:19: 'For what I do is not the good I want to do; no, the evil I do not want to do – this I keep on doing.' You live through the frustration of every day knowing that there will be something you will say today that is going to hurt somebody and there is going to be a thought going through your mind you ought not to have thought about because you are bound, as it were, locked into this humanity that is inhibited by sin. Well, imagine stepping out of it, imagine being released from it, imagine never saying ever again a hurtful word, or thinking a lustful thought, or wanting to do an evil deed. Imagine the liberation of being able to live without feeling sorry for or guilty about anything. Perfect holiness.

But there will also be *perfect love*. At the end of John 17, Jesus speaks of his people experiencing the very same love with which the Father has loved the Son. He talks about the final unity that comprehends the Father, the Son and the people of God, all in the love of God. That love is not only beyond our experience at present, it is also beyond our imagining and even our comprehension. Our love at the moment is imperfect, it vacillates, it is selective. But on that day we shall be able to love as Jesus loves, perfectly and without wavering.

In addition there will be *perfect wholeness*. This will be our experience on that day, because the experience as I said, will touch not only our spirits, but our bodies will also be transformed by it. I like these words of Paul in Philippians 3:20, where he says that 'we eagerly await a Saviour from heaven, the Lord Jesus Christ, who by the power that enables him to bring everything under his control, will transform our lowly bodies so that they will be like his glorious body'. Paul knew all about a lowly body, just as you and I do. He knew what it was to be hampered by frailty and sickness, exhaustion, even death. Paul knew what it was to have a thorn in the flesh, from which he found no relief in spite of prayer.

But the promise of Christ's return is the promise of a regenerated body, which will be a suitable vehicle for our renewed spirit. Just imagine it: Christ returns. We are caught up to be with him, and in the catching up, a transformation occurs that affects me both inwardly and outwardly. It transforms everything that held me back and kept me down and locked me into this space-time continuum of birth, life and death. It releases me.

When Jesus comes back, he will do more than clear away a headache or give relief from back pain. The crippled child will walk again; the defective mind will think clearly; the congenitally blind will see; the profoundly deaf will hear; the chronically ill will be healed, fully, finally and forever with undreamed of new powers with which to live, built to last as long as God lasts. The miracles of Jesus were just like the little flowers in springtime to herald the coming of that day of perfect wholeness when we awake in his presence. The return of Jesus will mark the ultimate experience.

3. The return of Jesus will produce the ultimate environment

While we are coping with the transformation inside us and outside us, and while we are coping with the sight of Jesus himself, we shall become eye-witnesses to another staggering sight. It is called by Peter in Acts 3:21 the 'renewal of all things', it is the time when God restores everything. It is the occasion Paul talks of in Romans 8:21, when the universe will be liberated from its bondage to decay at the coming of a new heaven and a new earth.

We all know about environmental damage and pollution, of ozone depletion; we all know about nature red in tooth and claw; we all know about the freaks of nature and the fungi and the weeds. But there, before our eyes, on that occasion, will be a transformation. Paradise will be restored.

The Bible has a lot to say about it.

In Isaiah 11, for example: 'The wolf will live with the lamb, the leopard will lie down with the goat, the calf and the lion and the yearling together; and a little child will lead them. The cow will feed with the bear, their young will lie down together, and the lion will eat straw like the ox. The infant will play near the hole of the cobra, and the young child put his hand into the viper's nest. They will neither harm nor destroy on all my holy mountain, for the earth will be full of the knowledge of the

Lord, as the waters cover the sea.'
  Or Isaiah 35:1-10:

    The desert and the parched land will be glad;
        the wilderness will rejoice and blossom.
    Like the crocus, it will burst into bloom;
        it will rejoice greatly and shout for joy.
    The glory of Lebanon will be given to it,
        the splendour of Carmel and Sharon;
    they will see the glory of the LORD,
        the splendour of our God.
    Strengthen the feeble hands,
        steady the knees that give way;
    say to those with fearful hearts,
        'Be strong, do not fear;
    your God will come,
        he will come with vengeance;
    with divine retribution
        he will come to save you.'
    Then will the eyes of the blind be opened
        and the ears of the deaf unstopped.
    Then will the lame leap like a deer,
        and the mute tongue shout for joy.
    Water will gush forth in the wilderness
        and streams in the desert.
    The burning sand will become a pool,
        the thirsty ground bubbling springs.
    In the haunts where jackals once lay,
        grass and reeds and papyrus will grow.
    And a highway will be there;
        it will be called the Way of Holiness.

The unclean will not journey on it;
  it will be for those who walk in that Way;
  wicked fools will not go about on it.
 No lion will be there,
  nor will any ferocious beast get up on it;
  they will not be found there.
But only the redeemed will walk there,
  and the ransomed of the LORD will return.
They will enter Zion with singing;
  everlasting joy will crown their heads.
Gladness and joy will overtake them,
  and sorrow and sighing will flee away.

Or take this picture in Revelation 21, where John caught up to heaven, sees a new heaven and a new earth and 'the Holy City, the new Jerusalem, coming down out of heaven from God, prepared as a bride beautifully dressed for her husband.

'And I heard a loud voice from the throne saying, "Now the dwelling of God is with men, and he will live with them. They will be his people, and God himself will be with them and be their God.

'He will wipe every tear from their eyes. There will be no more death or mourning or crying or pain, for the old order of things has passed away".'

There will be no more fatal accidents, no more incurable diseases, no more funeral services and no more final farewells; a perfect place, and possibly whole new worlds, a universe, to discover.

But notice all of those things were about earth, about here. There is continuity, there is familiarity about this Christian hope. It is not buzzing around in the sky among clouds somewhere, with harps. No, the Christian hope is a very concrete hope.

It will be a perfect world and a perfect people, because we are going to be there with others. Take the example of Jesus and his resurrection when people recognised him; or his references to Abraham, Isaac and Jacob. These all suggest that we will recognise each other there. Caught up, then, but caught up with others, suddenly conscious that we are with other people and that somehow the frustrations and the disappointments and the inadequacies and the weaknesses and the things that build barriers between people have all been removed. Isn't that glorious?

Muslim believers and Christian believers in Lebanon reconciled on that day. Catholic believers and Protestant believers reconciled on that day. All prejudices gone, as believers in Jesus Christ from whichever part of the world, from which ever tradition they have come to Christ, are caught up together. What an international gathering that will be, as we meet people from every tribe, and nation and race. With all the hang-ups and handicaps that hinder our relationships removed, there will be undreamed of possibilities for loving and lasting friendships. Nobody will be lonely on that day.

The return of Christ will produce the ultimate environment. We are going to see it.

4. The return of Christ will produce the ultimate enjoyment

The presence of Christ is invariably related to the theme of joy. No happiness we have ever known in our lives will come near to the joy of Christ's return. Do you notice how often in Jesus' parables, he likens the kingdom of God to a party, a banquet, a feast, where people make merry and are glad and enjoy the host, and his provision?

Have you noticed what it is to which the Lord's Table points us forward? It points us forward to the marriage feast of the Lamb. The kingdom of God is a party! It will be a time for celebration. The Psalmist writes, in Psalm 16:11: 'You will fill me with joy in your presence, with eternal pleasures at your right hand.' We will understand why it was that when they were drawing up the Shorter Catechism, they had as the first question - What is the chief end of man? Why does man exist? Man exists in order that he might glorify God and enjoy him for ever. The ultimate enjoyment.

5. The return of Christ will enlist us in the ultimate employment

The one thing you can say about Christ's return is that it will not be boring.

Think what is promised to us in the Bible. Very often the Bible speaks of an 'inheritance' (Matthew 25:34) - what are we to inherit? 2 Timothy 4:8 speaks of a crown of righteousness - that has to do with governing something. In Hebrews 2:5 ff. we are told that God has put aside, or prepared, the world to come, that is the universe to come - the new heavens, the planets and the stars, and the new earth - he has put it aside and prepared it, not for angels, but for us who are the children of God. Peter calls it the inheritance that can never perish, spoil or fade.

What are we going to do there? In Revelation 7:15, we are told that Christians 'are before the throne of God and they serve him'. In 1 Corinthians 6:2, Paul tells us something even more remarkable: 'Do you not know that the saints will judge the world? Do you not know that we will judge angels?' In other words, the destiny of a Christian believer is that they will rule with Christ, over the universe, and over the angelic beings. And with the whole universe at our feet, the whole of eternity at our disposal, there are no limits to the adventures we can have, to the achievements we can accomplish, to the creativity we can express, to the fulfilment we can enjoy. When Jesus comes again, it's going to be mind-blowing! It's all going to happen in an instant, without any time-delay, in the twinkling of an eye, at the last trumpet.

When Jesus comes again, it will mean all of this to the believer, *and much more*. For there is something that will surpass all of this but which you will not understand unless you are a Christian believer. It is summed up at the end of John 17, where Jesus says that when he comes again, we shall both see him, and be with him. Revelation 22:4 says: 'They will see God's face.' 1 John 3:2 says: 'We shall see him as he is.' The old Puritan writers used to call this the Beatific Vision, the beautiful vision, for we shall see God. The vision of Christ will be the vision of God.

There we must hold our breath for there can be no beauty more beautiful, there can be no loveliness more lovely, there can be no strength more strong, there can be no tenderness more tender, no majesty more majestic, no peace more peaceful, no joy more joyful, than this. We shall see him and be with him, with Jesus, the most significant Person in the universe. We will see the scars on his brow from the thorns, and the marks in his wrists from the nails. We will feel his eye as it lightens on us as individuals. We will hear him say, 'Hi, John, Hi, Mary, it is good to have you home at last.'

One hymn writer put it like this:

> Face to face with Christ my Saviour
> Face to face, what will it be?
> When with rapture I behold him
> Jesus Christ who died for me.

From our hearts, in anticipation of that day, there should well up within us the prayer that John wrote at the end of the book of Revelation: *Even so, come, Lord Jesus*.

And now, dear children, continue in him, so that when he appears we may be confident and unashamed before him at his coming. If you know that he is righteous, you know that everyone who does what is right has been born of him. How great is the love the Father has lavished on us, that we should be called children of God! And that is what we are! The reason the world does not know us is that it did not know him. Dear friends, now we are children of God, and what we will be has not yet been made known. But we know that when he appears, we shall be like him, for we shall see him as he is. Everyone who has this hope in him purifies himself, just as he is pure (1 John 2:28 -3:3).